THE DRAMATIC WORLD OF HAROLD PINTER

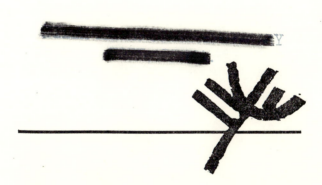

THE DRAMATIC WORLD
OF HAROLD PINTER:
ITS BASIS IN RITUAL

By *Katherine H. Burkman*

Ohio State University Press

For my mother
and in memory of my father

CONTENTS

ACKNOWLEDGMENTS

I would like to thank Dr. John C. Morrow and Dr. Roy H. Bowen for their sympathetic interest and invaluable assistance throughout my work. My thanks are also due to Dr. Edwin W. Robbins for his very helpful criticism; to Dr. Charles C. Ritter, through whom I first became interested in the role of myth and ritual in literature; and to Mr. and Mrs. Jack Ellison, whose initial fostering of my interest in drama and anthropology have led to this combined study.

I am grateful too for a scholarship from the General Development Fund of the Ohio State University that enabled me to participate in a London seminar in British theater history and to collect important data for my study in London. I am deeply indebted to Mr. Martin Esslin for his kindness in speaking with me about Mr. Pinter's drama and for making it possible to listen to recordings of Pinter's radio drama at the B.B.C. and to Miss Joan Kemp-Welch, Mr. Clive Donner, and Mr. Lawrence Pressman for their very helpful interviews, as well as to Dr. E. R. Howard Malpas for permission to quote from his dissertation. Appreciation is extended to the staff of the Enthoven Collection at the Victoria and Albert Museum; to the staff of the Library of the British Film Institute; and to the staff of the British Institute of Recorded Sound; to Associated Rediffusion Ltd. for the opportunity to see a rerun of *The Lover*; and to The British Film Institute for the opportunity to see the film of *The Caretaker*.

I wish to thank Methuen & Co., Ltd., and Grove Press for permission to quote from the works of Harold Pinter. I also wish to thank Faber and Faber Ltd. and Grove Press for permission to quote from Beckett's *Waiting for Godot*. I am grateful to Ivan Foxwell Productions Ltd. and The Rank Organization for permission to quote from "The Quiller Memorandum." The editors of *Modern Drama* have kindly permitted me to use, in somewhat altered form, my article "Pinter's A Slight Ache as Ritual" (December, 1968), which appears as chapter three of this book. I am grateful to the University of Nebraska Press for permission to quote from *Myth and Symbol: Critical Approaches and Applications*, and *Myth and Literature: Contemporary Theory and Practice*. I also wish to extend thanks to the editors of the *Saturday Review* for permission to quote from "Disobedience, Civil and Uncivil," by Henry Hewes (October 28, 1967); the *Humanist* for permission to quote from "The Decade of Harold Pinter," by Roger Manvell (32 [1967]); the *New Yorker* for permission to quote from "Two People in a Room" (February 25, 1967); and the *Nation* for permission to quote from "The Theatre," by Harold Clurman (23 [1967]).

My especial thanks are extended to Miss Peggy Waterkeyn at the Society of Film and Television Arts for her help; to Mr. Roger Manvell for his interview and his kind assistance with my research; to Mrs. Lucia Robinson and Mrs. Susan Collins for their editorial assistance; and to Dr. Roger Pierce, Mr. Frank Rodriquez, and Mrs. Madeleine Grumet for their helpful suggestions. Finally, I would like to thank Professor Robert M. Estrich for his kind interest and very helpful criticism.

Harold Pinter was born in 1930 and grew up in Hackney, a working-class area in the East End of London. His parents were Jewish, his father a tailor and an air-raid warden during the war. During the war years the boy was evacuated to the country twice; at other times, he would open the back door to find his garden in flames.

Although such exterior threats would be enough to make the playwright "the morose little boy"[1] he says he was, the anti-semitic atmosphere of Hackney was as threatening as the war. According to Charles Marowitz, "Pinter remembers scary walks through ill-lit alleys with ornery-looking toughs standing around clutching broken milk bottles."[2]

Pinter refused military service as a conscientious objector, studied briefly at the Royal Academy of Dramatic Art, and in 1949 became a repertory actor under the name of David Baron. He toured Ireland for eighteen months with Anew McMaster and later toured England with Sir Donald Wolfit. As a young actor, Pinter read modern novels, wrote poetry and prose pieces, and was an early admirer of Samuel Beckett.

He met the actress Vivien Merchant on tour and married her in 1956. She was later to create brilliant interpretations of some of her husband's heroines, such as Sarah in *The Lover* and Ruth in *The Homecoming*. Working at many jobs, from caretaker to doorman at a dancehall, Pinter wrote his first play, a one-acter called *The Room*, in 1957 on commission from a friend at the University of Bristol drama department. *The Birthday Party* soon followed but did not find a large public until Joan Kemp-Welch's television production of it. Though critical response to this production was mixed, beneath the reactions of shock, confusion, praise, and blame ran a strain of universal amazement at the power of the drama. Since that time, Pinter's dramatic world has remained an area of considerable critical interest and dispute.

Pinter has subsequently written scripts for radio, television, and film, as well as revue sketches, one-act plays, and two more full-length dramas for the theater. Active too as an actor and director, he is, in short, very much a man of the theater. He now lives with his wife and son Daniel in a five-story, period house overlooking London's Regent Park. Though not politically committed, he has associated himself with two causes: "I'm categorically anti the Americans in Viet Nam. And I feel strongly in favour of Israel."[3]

When still in his thirties, Pinter spoke of life with the weariness of age. "It's a short life. And I have no wish to be eighty-eight. I feel pretty exhausted now that I'm thirty-six,"[4] the playwright told an interviewer on a visit to New

York. Although he insisted that he could enjoy life greatly, his reflections on its burdensome nature help account for his sympathetic treatment of the characters that populate his dramas. "It's very difficult to feel contempt for others when you see yourself in the mirror," he commented in the same interview.[5]

The insecurity of Pinter's wartime childhood in Hackney, his subsequent lonely existence as a traveling actor living in furnished rooms and seaside boarding houses, the endless jobs that the acting life imposed, all may have contributed to the sense of menace and the theme of dispossession that dominate his dramatic world. The theme, moreover, continues to draw him. When entering a more successful phase of his playwrighting career in 1960, he spoke nostalgically of the time he spent, and had time to spend, at Fleet-Street's milk bar in the East End, listening to the talk of the kind of dispossessed people who appear in his revue sketches and waiting for the all-night bus. "The all-night buses used to fascinate me," he said. "They still do. The way they connect. The way you can get anywhere."[6]

Not all his critics like Harold Pinter's dramas or agree with the world view they contain, but the majority consider him an important playwright. He is often cited as the most original writer in England today and as one of the most significant of all living modern dramatists. In 1967 Harold Clurman said of him, for example:

> I do not see life as Pinter does. But it is imperative that he reveal his view of it; it is part of the truth. He is an artist, one of the most astute to have entered upon the world stage in the past ten years. Those who do not respect and appreciate his talent understand little of our times or its theatre.[7]

THE DRAMATIC WORLD OF HAROLD PINTER

1

Introduction

In art, in myth, and in ritual
man symbolizes his position of mystery
vis-à-vis the universe.[1]

The drama of Harold Pinter evolves in an atmosphere of mystery. While the surfaces of life are realistically detailed, the patterns below the surface are as obscure as the motives of the characters, the pause as prominent and suggestive as the dialogue. Despite the vivid naturalism of his characters' conversations, they behave very often more like figures in a dream than people with whom one can easily identify, at least on superficial levels.

Up to a point, Pinter himself is an excellent if reluctant guide to his mysterious dramatic world. "If you press me for a definition, I'd say that what goes on in my plays is realistic, but what I'm doing is not realism."[2] Here the playwright points to what his audience has so often sensed as distinctive in his style: its mixture of the real and the surreal, its exact portrayal of life on the surface, and its powerful evocation of that life which lies beneath the surface. His plays, Pinter suggests, are about "the weasel under the cocktail cabinet."[3]

Ominous undercurrents lurk, for example, beneath the most mundane exchanges over the breakfast table of the lower-class Meg and Petey in *The Birthday Party* or the upper-class Flora and Edward in *A Slight Ache*.

> MEG: Is that you, Petey?
> *Pause.*
> Petey, is that you?
> *Pause.*
> Petey?
> PETEY: What?
> MEG: Is that you?
> PETEY: Yes, it's me.
> MEG: What? (*Her face appears at the hatch.*) Are you back?
> PETEY: Yes.
> MEG: I've got your cornflakes ready. (*She disappears and reappears.*)
> Here's your cornflakes.
> *He rises and takes the plate from her, sits at the table, props up the paper and begins to eat. Meg enters by the kitchen door.*
> Are they nice?
> PETEY: Very nice.
> MEG: I thought they'd be nice. (*She sits at the table.*) You got your paper?
> PETEY: Yes.[4]

> FLORA: Have you noticed the honeysuckle this morning?
> EDWARD: The what?
> FLORA: The honeysuckle.
> EDWARD: Honeysuckle? Where?
> FLORA: By the backgate, Edward.
> EDWARD: Is that honeysuckle? I thought it was . . . convolvulus, or something.

FLORA: But you know it's honeysuckle.
EDWARD: I tell you I thought it was convolvulus.
  Pause.
FLORA: It's in wonderful flower.
EDWARD: I must look.[5]

The now famous Pinter pause, which punctuates the breakfast conversations of these two couples, heightens the effect of noncommunication which Pinter's observant ear records and his pen so readily and amusingly orchestrates, whether the focus be cornflakes or honeysuckle. The repetitions and lack of logic of ordinary conversation that the tightly knit realistic play so rarely includes are carefully woven into the texture of Pinter's dramatic world and give it its distinctive combination of the banal and the strange.

As the Pinter dialogue continues, however, the weasel gradually emerges from under the cocktail cabinet. Invariably the trivia of the characters' lives fails to save them from the sacrificial acts which are at the center of the action. At the end of *The Birthday Party* Meg and Petey still converse over the breakfast table, but the play has revolved around the sacrifice of Meg's beloved boarding house guest Stanley who has been "taken away." At the end of *A Slight Ache,* Flora continues to discuss the flowers in her garden, but she now addresses the silent matchseller who has emerged from his threatening position at the back gate to usurp her husband's position in his home.

But if the mysterious emerges and takes over in Pinter's drama, it is never completely explained. The nameless terror which threatens the Pinter hero is not fully identified, the mystery never resolved in the manner of an Ibsen. Although Goldberg and McCann take Stanley away in *The Birthday Party,* we never know why or whose orders they act upon. The absurd demands of the voice in *The Dumb Waiter,* are followed by the frightened killers, Gus and Ben; but the source of the orders is nameless. In *The*

Homecoming, Ruth decides to make her home with her husband's family rather than with her husband and children, but we are given no explicit reason for her choice.

An audience unused to unresolved mystery in its drama is naturally baffled and threatened by such withholding of information. Some of his critics have accused Pinter of willful mystification, skipping every other line of a normal conversation, or deliberately keeping the audience in the dark. Others have found his characters too grotesque or special to be relevant. "The more acute the experience the less articulate its expression,"[6] is Pinter's own defense of his technique. The playwright does not seek to mystify or puzzle his audience; he merely explores experience at levels which are mysterious and which preclude the kind of clear explanation of life which the tradition of the well-made play has often delivered in the form of thesis or message. Not interested in the political concerns of such contemporaries as Osborne or Wesker, Pinter prefers to explore his characters as they appear "at the extreme edge of their living, where they are living pretty much alone."[7] As Martin Esslin suggests, Pinter's exploration of that in life which is not easily verifiable leads him back to such essentials in drama as "the suspense created by the elementary ingredients of pure, pre-literary theatre; a stage, two people, a door; a poetic image of an undefined fear and expectation."[8]

Esslin's placement of the playwright among the poetic absurdists offers an important clue to an understanding of Pinter's dramatic world. The absurdist dramatists, he suggests, are no longer telling stories but exploring states of being and revealing patterns. In such plays one is no longer interested in what is transpiring in the present: one is concerned, rather, with the nature of the unfolding pattern or poetic image. The theatre of the absurd, writes Esslin, demands a response similar to that given to abstract painting, sculpture, or poetry. It grips the spectator "both on the level of the archetypel image that strikes chords in the deepest layers of the mind and on the level of a highly intellectual interpretive effort."[9]

Esslin sees the shift from the well-made play to the absurdist poetic play as a reflection of man's sense of the absurdity of existence, his feeling of existential anguish. He defines the absurdist technique as existentialist in form as well as in content—a general breaking up of a rational order of event, character, and setting to better reflect the world as it is perceived.[10] Walter Kerr goes a step farther and reserves the existentialist technique for Pinter alone. Only Pinter, he insists, "does not simply content himself with restating a handful of existential themes inside familiar forms of playmaking. He remakes the play altogether so that it will function according to existential principle."[11]

According to Kerr, even Samuel Beckett presents his images as concept, whereas Pinter involves us in a Kafkaesque world of anxiety—in a concrete world of present realities in which the pattern eludes and involves us.[12] While we seek the conceptual "nub" in a Beckett play, in the world of Pinter's drama "we give existence free rein, accept it as primary, refrain from demanding that it answer our questions, grant it the mystery of not yet having named itself."[13]

At the same time, however, that Pinter's art reflects the mysterious universe as he perceives it, it also attempts to approach the mystery that it reflects. Kerr's irritation with Pinter when the writer seems to betray "a belief in essential nature"[14] reveals the critic's bias rather than the playwright's weakness. Though Pinter is distinctly a poetic rather than a problem-solving playwright, he is by his own proud admission in large part a traditionalist. Despite his lack of certain kinds of explicit information about his characters and plot, in form Pinter is not as far from the well-made play of Ibsen as many of his fellow absurdists; he is fond of curtain lines and curtains, and he is ultimately concerned with the shape both of words and of his entire dramatic world. "For me everything has to do with shape, structure, and over-all unity,"[15] Pinter noted in an interview—a statement which does not contradict his assertion that his creative process is not conceptual, that he follows his characters whither they lead him.[16]

The point is that Pinter's characters lead him continually to the very rhythmic structures which have informed great dramatic works since drama's origin in primitive ritual. Rather than focusing on lack of communication, Pinter concerns himself with the way people fail to avoid that communication from which they wish to run. While other absurdist writers often allow their characters to succeed in avoiding communication, Pinter's dramatic world is one of action in the old Aristotelian sense of the word. The playwright himself is aware of the movement toward communication in his work and its dramatic finality.

> We have heard many times that tired, grimy phrase, "failure of communication," and this phrase has been fixed to my work consistently. I believe the contrary. I think that we communicate only too well in our silence, in what is unsaid, and that what takes place is continual evasion, desperate rearguard attempts to keep ourselves to ourselves. . . . I'm not suggesting that no character in a play can ever say what in fact he means. Not at all. I have found that there invariably does come a moment when this happens, where he says something, perhaps, which he has never said before. And where this happens, what he says is irrevocable, and can never be taken back.[17]

Pinter goes on to describe his own struggle with communication and the nature of that territory he chooses to explore. Words, he says, both please and discourage him, almost to the point of nausea. The bulk of them so often become "a stale dead terminology" that it is very easy to be overcome by paralysis. "But if it is possible to confront this nausea, to follow it to its hilt and move through it, then it is possible to say that something has occurred, that something has even been achieved."[18]

> Language, under these conditions, is a highly ambiguous commerce. So often, below the words spoken, is the thing known and unspoken. My characters tell me so much and no more, with reference to their experience, their aspirations, their motives, their history. Between my lack of biographical data about them and the ambiguity of what they say there lies a territory which is not only worthy of exploration but which it is compulsory to explore. You and I, the characters which grow on a page, most of the time we're inexpressive, giving little away, unreliable, elusive, evasive, obstructive, unwilling. But it's out of these attributes that a language arises. A language, I repeat, where, underneath what is said, another thing is being said.[19]

The distinction between problem and mystery is a helpful one for an approach to the hidden language and nameless weasel of Pinter's drama. In mystery, the objective and the subjective merge. While man confronts problems in life, he is a part of life's mysteries. In Pinter's one-act play, *A Slight Ache*, Edward puzzles over a matchseller who hovers continually at his back gate. When he invites the matchseller in, the middle-aged Englishman comes to feel a strange kinship with him: problem gives way to mystery as Edward realizes his own involvement in the action. The matchseller is never realistically identified. He doesn't speak a single word in the entire play. Still, the play's action reveals Edward approaching the stranger and finally in absolute imitation exchanging places with him. Like the savage who realizes that "a breach of alienation between himself and the universe" can be only intermittently closed, "not closed in actuality, but mimetically,"[20] Edward approaches the matchseller and assumes his role. Only in this way can he approach the mysterious depths in himself which he has feared and now is forced to accept.

If man may close the gap between himself and the mysterious universe only mimetically, not actually, through ritual, myth, and art,[21] Pinter has availed himself of all three methods of imitation in his drama. Just as the primitive rites of ancient religions work their way into the structure of art, in drama as notably as in painting and sculpture, ritual becomes part of Pinter's dramatic world, in which it is used for the playwright's own tragi-comic purposes.

A reading of Pinter's plays in the light of the ritual rhythms which structure them involves an understanding of two distinct kinds of rituals which the playwright sets in counterpoint with each other. On the one hand, the plays abound in those daily habitual activities which have become formalized as ritual and have tended to become empty of meaning, an automatic way of coping with life. These automatic and meaningless activities contrast in the plays with echoes of sacred sacrificial rites which are loaded with meaning and force the characters into an awareness of life from which their daily activities have helped to protect them. My contention is that beneath the daily secular rituals which Pinter weaves into the texture of his plays—"the taking of a toast and tea"—beat the rhythms of ancient fertility rites, which form a significant counterpoint to the surface rituals of the plays and which often lend the dramas their shape and structure.

John Russell Brown notes Pinter's concern with secular, everyday ceremonies of social activity that have become formalized or frozen into patterns of social behavior. He remarks on Pinter's continued interest in such rituals, "from a birthday party to a homecoming, through seeking living space, taking possession, or taking 'care' of a room, to taking breakfast or lunch, taking orders, fulfilling routines, visiting, collecting, and so on."[22] Hugh Nelson also notes the revelation of family stress in *The Homecoming* through "the small rituals of family living: breakfast, tea, dusting, opening and closing windows."[23]

The opening of Pinter's first one-act play, *The Room*, offers an excellent example of the author's typical use of such daily rituals.

> *Bert is at the table, wearing a cap, a magazine propped in front of him. Rose is at the stove.*
>
> ROSE: Here you are. This'll keep the cold out.
> *She places bacon and eggs on a plate, turns off the gas and takes the plate to the table.*
> It's very cold out, I can tell you. It's murder.
> *She returns to the stove and puts water from the kettle into the teapot, turns off the gas and brings the teapot to the table, pours salt and sauce on the plate and cuts two slices of bread. Bert begins to eat.*
> That's right. You eat that. You'll need it. You can feel it in here. Still, the room keeps warm. It's better than the basement, anyway.
> *She butters the bread.*
> I don't know how they live down there. It's asking for trouble. Go on. Eat it up. It'll do you good.
> *She goes to the sink, wipes a cup and saucer and brings them to the table.*
> If you want to go out you might as well have something inside you. Because you'll feel it when you get out.
> *She pours milk into the cup.*
> Just now I looked out of the window. It was enough for me. There wasn't a soul about. Can you hear the wind?
> *She sits in the rocking-chair.*
> I've never seen who it is. Who is it? Who lives down there? I'll have to ask. I mean, you might as well know, Bert. But whoever it is, it can't be too cozy.
> *Pause.*
> I think it's changed hands since I was last there. I didn't see who moved in then. I mean the first time it was taken.
> *Pause.*
> Anyway, I think they've gone now.
> *Pause.*
> But I think someone else has gone in now. I wouldn't like to live in that basement. Did you ever see the walls? They were running. This is all right for me. Go on, Bert. Have a bit more bread.

She goes to the table and cuts a slice of bread.
I'll have some cocoa on when you come back.
She goes to the window and settles the curtain.
No, this room's all right for me. I mean, you know where
you are. When it's cold, for instance.[24]

As Rose continues her virtual monologue, the breakfast
ritual becomes a desperate attempt on her part to sustain
her life with her husband, to protect them both from all
that is outside the room, whether it be the weather, the
dangerous environment of the basement, or the possible
strangers—"foreigners"—who may inhabit it. The repeti-
tiveness of the dialogue, its constant references to the
warmth of the room and the dangers without, suggest an
unspoken fear of some unnamed danger.

As in the rest of Pinter's dramatic world, the rituals of
daily life are seen at one and the same time as comic and
ineffectual, and as tragic and pathetic. Their emptiness is
exposed with all the intellectuality of Ionesco's kind of
irony, but the effort to sustain them is explored with all
the sympathy of Beckett for his two *Godot* clowns, desperately improvising their routines in a void. But in *The Room*,
as in all Pinter's dramas, the secular ritual is set in tension
with a more primitive religious rite. The "foreigner" does
emerge from the basement. He is killed by Rose's returning husband, and Rose is stricken blind. Action occurs.
The secular rituals are unable to protect Rose from the sacrificial rite that climaxes the play and destroys forever the
security of the room.

At the center of the action of most Pinter plays is the
pharmakos, or scapegoat, of ancient ritual and tragedy, the
victim whose destruction serves in a special way to re-
establish certain basic relationships in the family or com-
munity. Hugh Nelson considers Teddy, the returning son
in *The Homecoming*, as such a victim. "The ostensible hero
is transformed," he writes, "into a pharmakos, or scapegoat, a transformation with which we are familiar from
Pinter's earlier plays."[25] Indeed, Nelson's reading of *The*

Homecoming suggests his understanding of Pinter's use of secular daily rituals and sacred primitive ones in counterpoint as he describes how the veneer of civilization in that drama gives way to the primitive elements below the surface. He writes:

> The concept of family which Max and Lenny have is clearly a collage of empty clichés . . . but beneath the verbal gloss, as beneath a politician's pancreas, what we see in the attitudes and response of the characters and in their relationships to each other is a reality which is prehistoric and primitive, a world where appetite reigns.[26]

It is possible, of course, to explore the ritual basis of almost any work of dramatic art, and of much nondramatic art as well. The school of "myth critics," which has arisen in modern times and followed in the footsteps of James Frazer and the Cambridge school of anthropologists, has explored the close connection between ritual, myth, and art.

With Jane E. Harrison's publication of *Themis* in 1912, the theory of the Cambridge anthropologists that ritual precedes myth, that myths indeed are verbalizations of rituals, became generally available.[27] The theory was later endorsed by the influential philosopher Ernst Cassirer, who believed that "man acts first and rationalizes his conduct later."[28] Although definitions of myth vary widely and debate rages amid anthropologists and the recent breed of literary anthropologists as to whether ritual or myth came first, Clyde Kluckhohn's dismissal of the debate as meaningless seems most clarifying. Stress should rather be put, writes this renowned anthropologist, on "the intricate interdependence of myth (which is one form of ideology) with ritual and many other forms of behavior."[29] Kluckhohn goes on to explain:

> Those realms of behavior and of experience which man finds beyond rational and technological control he feels are capable of manipulation through symbols. Both myth and rit-

ual are symbolical procedures and are most closely tied together by this, as well as by other, facts. The myth is a system of word symbols, whereas ritual is a system of object and act symbols. Both are symbolic processes for dealing with the same type of situation in the same affective mode.[30]

Kluckhohn further comments on the common psychological basis of myth and ritual.

Rituals and myths supply, then, fixed points in a world of bewildering change and disappointment. . . . For myth and ritual have a common psychological basis. Ritual is an obsessive repetitive activity—often a symbolic dramatization of the fundamental "needs" of the society, whether "economic," "biological," "social," or "sexual." Mythology is the rationalization of those same needs, whether they are all expressed in overt ceremonial or not.[31]

Those critics concerned with the connections between myth and literature have recognized the inevitable and productive relationships between ritual and myth and the arts. The artist, like the primitive myth-maker, seeks to envision a basic unity in life, to deny death, and to affirm life. He too works through symbols and shares with the primitive myth-maker a desire, albeit often unconscious, to "promote social solidarity as well as solidarity with nature as a whole in time of social crisis."[32]

Like the ritualist and the myth-maker, too, the artist allows the irrational its province. Joseph Campbell writes that myth "is dreamlike and, like dream, a spontaneous product of the psyche; like dream, revelatory of the psyche and hence of the whole nature and destiny of man."[33] The myth critic, following Jung, believes that the primitive still lurks in the most civilized of men who, despite the advances of science, "recreates nightly in his dreams the primordial symbols of ancient myth."[34]

Pinter lends himself to ritual or mythical critical examination more than many of his contemporaries, partly because he focuses continually on the primitive qualities which lurk beneath the civilized veneer of modern life and erupt into that life, and partly because his determination to confront the mysterious, unsolvable regions of man's existence has led him into the realms of myth and ritual. The playwright disclaims any reading knowledge of anthropology,[35] and his myth-making qualities are not the self-conscious ones of the poet Yeats, who sought to write "not drama, but the ritual of a lost faith."[36] He becomes rather the daytime dreamer who is drawn to the same ritual patterns which Northrop Frye suggests have drawn men through the centuries to deal in similar archetypal patterns with the mystery of our being.

> Total literary history moves from the primitive to the sophisticated, and here we glimpse the possibility of seeing literature as a complication of a relatively restricted and simple group of formulas that can be studied in primitive culture. If so, then the search for archetypes is a kind of literary anthropology, concerned with the way that literature is informed by preliterary categories such as ritual, myth, and folk-tale. We next realize that the relation between these categories and literature is by no means purely one of descent, as we find them reappearing in the greatest classics— in fact there seems to be a general tendency on the part of great classics to revert to them. This coincides with a feeling that we have all had; that the study of mediocre works of art, however, energetic, obstinately remains a random and peripheral form of critical experience, whereas the profound masterpiece seems to draw us to a point at which we can see an enormous number of converging patterns of significance. Here we begin to wonder if we cannot see literature, not only as complicating itself in time, but as spread out in conceptual space from some unseen center.[37]

"How myth gets into literature is variously explained by the Jungian racial memory, historical diffusion, or the essential similarity of the human mind everywhere."[38] How ritual and myth get into literature or into Pinter's dramatic world is not a major object of concern in this study, but the influence of Frazer's pivotal mythical study, *The Golden Bough*, on modern literature gives some interesting cause for speculation. Whether Pinter is directly familiar with Frazer's classic, he is by his own admission widely read. The cyclical theory of culture which Frazer's book propounds has doubtless reached him through such writers as T. S. Eliot and James Joyce, who have made conscious and explicit use of Frazer's theories and images in their works. The ideas of Frazer, Harrison, and Murray are so much a part of the modern literary consciousness that Pinter could hardly have avoided an awareness of them.

John B. Vickery discusses Frazer's work as a modern myth on man's quest for survival, a literary work in its own right, which is actually "less a compendium of facts than a gigantic quest romance couched in the form of objective research."[39] Vickery believes that many modern writers have been deeply influenced by Frazer's work both in subject matter and approach. These writers not only share his focus on the scapegoat figure, and on death and resurrection, but "for them as well as for Frazer, harvesting, lovemaking, bearing the sins of others, and performing the menial deeds of daily life, all reflect in different ways what is taken to be the essence of life."[40] That essence, Vickery suggests, is discussed by Frazer, who "mediates between the external and internal worlds of Marx or Darwin and Freud"[41] and considers the individual and the land "the twin foci of man's endless battle for a viable existence, themes which have been as inexhaustible for modern literature as they have been imperative for modern life."[42]

The Golden Bough, then, with its rich storehouse of ritual and mythology, became "the discursive archetype and hence matrix" of twentieth-century literature, according to Vickery, because "it was grounded in the essential realism of anthropological research, informed with the romance quest of an ideal, and controlled by the irony in divine myth and human custom."[43] Certainly Frazer's *Golden*

Bough kings offer an excellent metaphorical clue to the ritual sacrifices at the center of Pinter's drama.

Pinter, then, as he consciously or unconsciously traces basic ritual patterns in his dramatic world, is reaching back over the centuries to archaic rhythms which have always dominated drama at its best. He is also treating those rhythms in a highly individual, even unique, way and is moving at the same time in the mainstream of much in modern literature which has already gained the stature of the classic and which is pressingly and seriously relevant to our times.

"If you press me for a definition, I'd say that what goes on in my plays is realistic, but what I'm doing is not realism."[44] What goes on in Pinter's plays is realistic, as he suggests; but if his drama is taken as realism alone, it is bound to appear grotesque. Taken as poetry it begins to make sense as image and pattern. Because the images and patterns of his drama are based in ritual, a study of the dramas' ritual counterpoint may well help to reveal what it is in Pinter's dramatic world that, as he also suggests, is "not realism." If Pinter's drama employs ritual to approach the mysteries of life, one may well in turn approach that drama through an attempt to understand his use of that ritual.

Two Variations on the Theme of *The Golden Bough*:
Victim and Victor as Victim

They give birth astride of a grave,
the light gleams an instant,
then it's night once more.[1]

We often bemoan the loss to modern drama of the tragic
hero. We seek in vain for that noble character whom Aristotle described, whose fall from great heights is balanced
by his spiritual strength and growth, whose suffering is in
excess of his deserts, but whose fall is due in part to his
own character. This tragic hero, victim of the fates and of
himself, carrying within him the seeds of his own doom
and of his spiritual triumph, the Prometheus of Aeschylus,
the Oedipus of Sophocles, the Hamlet of Shakespeare, has
been replaced in modern drama by a series of victims of
accident, society, or heredity, a series of little men whose
fall is not far, whose dignity is questionable, and whose
victories of insight are negligible.

Pinter, no less than Miller, Williams, Osborne, or Ionesco, presents us with the little man, with the victim rather than the victim-victor of heroic stature. In *The Birthday Party*, Stanley is in hiding from the world that descends upon him in the form of Goldberg and McCann. They proceed to demolish what little sense of identity this has-been-if-ever artist has mustered up and taken with him into hiding. In *The Caretaker*, a self-deceiving tramp, who has mislaid his identity in Sidcup along with his papers, loses through his own machinations what small refuge from the misfortunes of his life he has temporarily been able to achieve. In *The Dumb Waiter*, a hired killer is to be executed for reasons beyond his powers of comprehension; and in *A Slight Ache*, an effete Edward is replaced in his own elegant home by a voiceless and smelly match-seller who doesn't even sell matches. A play such as *Tea Party* would even seem to reverse the tragic rhythm as a man's rise in the business world is paralleled with his gradual disintegration as a human being.

Pinter's characters share with the characters of contemporary drama a lack of the redeeming sense of self which has permeated the truly tragic drama of the past. Modern drama, no less than ancient, is concerned with man's salvation, his redemption from the finality of death; but as it reflects man's loss of his sense of self, it reflects too his loss of a sense of order in the universe. The arbitrary nature of salvation baffles Vladimir in Beckett's *Waiting for Godot*, and he puzzles over the report by only one of the four evangelists that one of the two thieves crucified with Christ was saved. The nature of salvation, whether Godot will come, whether he indeed exists, is no clearer to Vladimir and Estragon than their own existence. "You're sure you saw me, you won't come and tell me to-morrow that you never saw me,"[2] Vladimir pleads with the emissary from Godot, no surer of his own identity than of Godot's identity or of the salvation which he seeks from Godot.

But if Pinter's world also reflects a loss of sense of self

and if its surface reflects the arbitrary nature of events, its rhythms suggest an order beneath the surface that connects with the rhythms of ancient tragedy and comedy as well as with their ritual base. A close look at Pinter's characters reveals a curious ambiguity about their positions as victims. Stanley, in *The Birthday Party*, is victimized by two men who are themselves frightened, potential victims of the power they serve. And Stanley becomes more than a victim when he attempts to strangle his landlady Meg and rape the visiting Lulu. Gus, the killer in *The Dumb Waiter*, is frightened: the killer must be killed. Edward, replaced by the matchseller, is clearly victim, but we see him as well in the course of *A Slight Ache* as the terrible killer—of a wasp. Ruth is clearly both victim and victor in her final role as prostitute in *The Homecoming*, which closes on the ambiguous question of who will be most exploited in the new family arrangements. In almost all of Pinter's plays, then, an ambiguity exists about the nature of the victim. He may not be the heroic victim-victor of ancient tragedy whose victory is often won on the spiritual plane, but he does share with his ancient brethren the double role of victim and victor.

Frazer's *The Golden Bough* has as its central myth the plight of a victim-victor which may well serve to illuminate the nature of Pinter's characters and their relationship to the tragic and comic dramas from which they descend. The Golden Bough is a bough of the tree of Diana's sacred grove in Nemi, which, Frazer explains, was broken off by the contenders to the priesthood of Nemi. Such a contender to the priesthood succeeded to the office by slaying the old priest, and he in turn was slain by the next contender. Frazer describes in dramatic terms the uneasy rule of the victor-victim priest.

> The post which he held by this precarious tenure carried with it the title of king; but surely no crowned head ever lay uneasier, or was visited by more evil dreams, than his. For

year in, year out, in summer and winter, in fair weather and in foul, he had to keep his lonely watch, and whenever he snatched a troubled slumber it was at the peril of his life. . . . The dreamy blue of Italian skies, the dappled shade of summer woods, and the sparkle of waves in the sun can have accorded but ill with that stern and sinister figure. Rather we picture to ourselves the scene as it may have been witnessed by a belated wayfarer on one of those wild autumn nights when the dead leaves are falling thick, and the winds seem to sing the dirge of the dying year.[3]

Frazer's entire book is an attempt to explain the priest-hood of Nemi, to find the universal rhythms that he believed beat beneath the strange surface of the custom. Itself a quest for the meaning of the strange succession to the priesthood, the book takes as its central theme the "victory of fertility over the waste land."[4] The priest-king of Nemi becomes the prototype of the succession of dying king-gods—Attis, Adonis, Dionysus, whose death and resurrection is celebrated in a vast variety of rituals that share a desire to preserve the god and his worshipers from death. In such rituals, as Gilbert Murray describes them, "the daiman is fought against and torn to pieces, announced as dead, wept for, collected and recognized, and revealed in his new divine light."[5]

The savage, Frazer notes, often regards his priest-king as a god. And since the death of such a man-god is unacceptable to him, he comes to believe that killing such a figure in his prime and transferring his soul to another will preserve that soul from death.[6] If degeneration of the priest-king could be prevented, primitive man felt he could insure safety from degeneration for mankind, for cattle, and for crops as well.[7] This sacrifice of the priest-king-god or of some substitute for him became associated in time with the sacrifice of a scapegoat, of one who could take upon him the sufferings and sins of the tribe.[8] (The meaning in primitive religious ritual of "scapegoat" receives a precise interpretation in the Old Testament account in Leviticus

16 in connection with the Hebrew Day of Atonement. Here a sacrificial goat laden with the confessed iniquities of the children of Israel was sent into the wilderness to Azazel with the implication that sin was cast out of the borders of the people. The principle of the scapegoat has been extraordinarily potent in historical Judaism.) Sometimes the fertility ritual was enacted as an *agon*, or battle, between a new god and an old god—the battle, for example, between the contenders for the priesthood of Nemi with the reigning priest. At other times a single god was the focus of the ritual; his sacrifice and resurrection, which Murray has described, suggest the same meanings of renewal, the same victory over death, the same ridding of the tribe of its own sins, which may be heaped upon the dying god as scapegoat.

Pinter's dramas may seem far from such questions of fertility ritual, of the sacrificing of god-kings to insure the continuance of life. Stanley, in *The Birthday Party*, is hardly the romantically described priest of Nemi, sword in hand, ready to defend his crown with his life. A strong parallel does exist, however; and Frazer's description of the menaced priest becomes an illuminating image for Pinter's dramatic world, especially for some of his earlier plays—*The Room* (1957), *The Birthday Party* (1957), *The Dumb Waiter* (1957), and *A Slight Ache* (1959), commonly referred to as comedies of menace—and his film, *The Quiller Memorandum* (1966).

The Birthday Party, for example, may be viewed as an *agon* between Stanley, who has challenged the reigning priest-king, and Monty, who has sent Goldberg and Mc-Cann to take care of the rebel. But Stanley is in hiding in *The Birthday Party* and must be forced into the play's *agon*.

On another level of the play's action Stanley is the sacrificed and resurrected god, the scapegoat king who is destroyed only to be reborn in the image of Monty. Here,

Stanley is a victim-victor; but since the entire action is shaped by Monty, even the resurrection gives the impression of victimization. Despite his double role of victim and victor in *The Birthday Party*, Stanley gives an overall impression of being a victim.

The name of Pinter's play, *The Birthday Party*, is in itself suggestive. Although Stanley emphatically denies that it is his birthday in the play, the celebration of his birth climaxes a drama that clearly leads the reluctant celebrant to his death, whether physical or spiritual. "They give birth astride of a grave, the light gleams an instant, then it's night once more."[9] Such is the fate of Stanley whose birth and death occur figuratively within a twenty-four-hour period, and such is the fate of the lonely and menaced priest of Nemi guarding his Golden Bough.

Unlike the priest, however, Stanley is hiding out from life in Meg and Petey's seaside boarding house; he is even hiding from Meg and Petey. He is reluctant to come down to breakfast, to see the birth of a new day.

MEG: Is Stanley up yet?
PETEY: I don't know. Is he?
MEG: I don't know. I haven't seen him down yet.
PETEY: Well, then, he can't be up.
MEG: Haven't you seen him down?
PETEY: I've only just come in.
MEG: He must be still asleep. (P. 10)

This amusingly banal interchange helps to introduce us to the over-motherly, hovering, and dense Meg and her dumbly patient husband; but we also come to see Stanley as reluctant to live. When Meg complains of how he goes through his socks, Petey makes Stanley's main pastime clear. "Why? He's in bed half the week" (p. 12). And yet Stanley claims that he hasn't slept at all. "Oh, God, I'm tired" (p. 19), he complains, obviously irritated with the flirtatious and hovering Meg and immediately alarmed at her announcement that two gentlemen may be coming to stay.

From the beginning of the play, Stanley behaves somewhat like a caged animal waiting for the slaughter. He attacks the breakfast of cornflakes, which Petey had listlessly praised when they were served to him by Meg as if they were a seven-course meal. Indeed, the daily rituals upon which Meg depends (one critic describes the breakfast with Petey as a litany with Meg as celebrant and Petey giving the responses[10]) irritate and disgust Stanley, who is overwhelmed with a sense of despair at his deliberately caged-in existence.

STANLEY: How long has that tea been in the pot?

MEG: It's good tea. Good strong tea.

STANLEY: This isn't tea. It's gravy.

MEG: It's not.

STANLEY: Get out of it. You succulent old washing bag.

MEG: I am not! And it isn't your place to tell me if I am!

STANLEY: And it isn't your place to come into a man's bedroom and—wake him up. (Pp. 18-19)

Stanley's plight at the play's opening is well described by Dr. Franzblau:

The play really begins with Stanley's coming downstairs. This is birth—not his birth alone, but birth in general. Petey is the father image—remote, shadowy, uninvolved, never there, never communicating with Stanley, reading his newspaper and minding his beach chairs. Meg is the universal, clinging, infantilizing, seductive "Mom"—the kind of mother who produces the Stanleys of life. From her, Stanley gets only illicit pleasure, infinite coddling, meanness, poverty of mind and emotion.

No wonder that his eyes have an already-dead-when-born look in them, and he never knows who he is or how to face reality with courage or energy. He looks out at the world frightened, weaving fantasies of accomplishment which bring him no comfort, having no truths to rely on, no friends, no road to travel. He knows only that he cannot accept the way of life of the Establishment—or blind his eyes with faith in God, man, or the future.[11]

Indeed, Stanley's own father is as shadowy as Petey. "My father nearly came down to hear me" (p. 23), Stanley explains to Meg as he describes his one successful concert as a pianist.

> Then after that, you know what they did? They carved me up. Carved me up. It was all arranged, it was all worked out. My next concert. Somewhere else it was. In winter. I went down there to play. Then, when I got there, the hall was closed, the place was shuttered up, not even a caretaker. (P. 23)

Stanley's story clearly foreshadows his role as the play's victim. His one concert, a success with champagne, was followed by the concert at which they "carved" him up by plan, a comic version of the tragic fall, the reversal of fortune. And here, too, figurative reference is made to the actual carving up of the scapegoat, a fate which Stanley will once more undergo in the play's action.

Shut out of life, silenced, carved up even before his "birth" in the play, Stanley's wavering sense of identity tests itself mainly in his outbursts with Meg. Frightened by the prospect of the gentlemen visitors, Stanley in turn terrifies Meg with the possibility that she may be carted away by the gentlemen who carry a wheelbarrow in their van for the purpose.

Even afraid to go outside, Stanley contemplates escape with the visiting Lulu, but he knows such escape is impossible.

> STANLEY: (*abruptly*). How would you like to go away with me?
> LULU: Where.
> STANLEY: Nowhere. Still, we could go.

LULU: But where could we go?
STANLEY: Nowhere. There's nowhere to go. So we could just go. It wouldn't matter. (P. 27)

The echoes from *Waiting for Godot* are significant. There is nowhere to go. Place and time have no meaning. "Have you not done tormenting me with your accursed time!" Pozzo scolds Vladimir in Beckett's play.

It's abominable! When! When! One day, is that not enough for you, one day he went dumb, one day I went blind, one day we'll go deaf, one day we were born, one day we shall die, the same day, the same second, is that not enough for you? (*Calmer.*) They give birth astride of a grave, the light gleams an instant, then it's night once more. (P. 57)

Time and space, however, have more meaning in *The Birthday Party*, in which the anguished waiting of Godot's world is replaced by a frightening sense of doom.

The sense of menace and doom in the play is partly expressed by Stanley's fear and partly by the constant patter of questions that are responded to with more questions rather than with answers.

STANLEY: No. Listen. (*Urgently.*) Has Meg had many guests staying in this house, besides me, I mean before me?
LULU: Besides you?
STANLEY (*impatiently*): Was she very busy, in the old days?
LULU: Why should she be?
STANLEY: What do you mean? This used to be a boarding house, didn't it?
LULU: Did it?
STANLEY: Didn't it?
LULU: Did it?
STANLEY: Didn't . . . oh, skip it. (P. 28)

Juxtaposed with Stanley's anxiety about space, about where he is, is that of McCann, one of the two men who descend on the boarding house to take Stanley away. Goldberg, his co-worker and apparent supervisor, responds to McCann's questions either with clichés about himself as a family man, with questions rather than answers, or with doubletalk.

> McCANN: Nat. How do we know this is the right house?
> GOLDBERG: What?
> McCANN: How do we know this is the right house?
> GOLDBERG: What makes you think it's the wrong house?
> McCANN: I didn't see a number on the gate.
> GOLDBERG: I wasn't looking for a number. (P. 29)

No more satisfied than Stanley about where he is, Mc-Cann anxiously questions Goldberg about the nature of their job and receives a baffling answer with which he must be satisfied.

> GOLDBERG: The main issue is a singular issue and quite distinct from your previous work. Certain elements, however, might well approximate in points of procedure to some of your other activities. All is dependent on the attitude of our subject. At all events, McCann, I can assure you that the assignment will be carried out and the mission accomplished with no excessive aggravation to you or myself. Satisfied?
> McCANN: Sure. Thank you, Nat. (P. 32)

By the end of act 1, Stanley has been awakened, been born, and been terrified with a sense of his death. When Meg announces his birthday to him and tells him of the party planned by the ominous Goldberg, Stanley denies that it is his birthday and beats the toy drum that Meg gives him as a gift "because you haven't got a piano" (p. 38). Stanley's subsequent march around the table beating the drum becomes more erratic and uncontrolled as he goes, until he arrives at Meg's chair, "his face and the drumbeat now savage and possessed" (p. 39), and the curtain falls.

In the light of a ritual reading, the events of act 1 are less mystifying than mysterious. Beneath the veneer of the seedy seaside resort, the primitive cycle is re-enacted. Stanley becomes "savage and possessed," his very being threatened by those to whom he would not at the moment of his brief victory as an artist "crawl down on . . . bended knees" (p. 24). The counterpoint of secular and sacred ritual is clear as the daily ceremony of awakening is played against the sacred rite of sacrifice, and the scapegoat is made ready.

At the birthday party itself, the hunted and hunter are one. The rhythm is a familiar one and finds its prototype not only in the victim-victor priests of Nemi but also in the scapegoat king, Oedipus, whom Sophocles portrays striking out viciously and irrationally at Creon and Tieresias once he has sensed his double position as victor (the solver of the riddle, the king, the savior of his people) and victim (both the contaminator of his land and the scapegoat—the incestuous murderer who must be banished).

The ceremonial atmosphere is created by the ritualistic tearing by McCann of a piece of newspaper into five equal strips, a prelude to the spiritual tearing apart of Stanley at the party. As Stanley attempts to escape, McCann blocks his exit, warning his victim at intervals not to disturb the torn strips which he fingers. The reluctant celebrant is further menaced by the affable cliché-ridden Goldberg and the brutal, but singing, McCann. And if Stanley fails to escape from "the terrorism of our world, so often embodied in false bonhomie and bigoted brutality,"[12] the horror of his plight is intensified by the unawareness of Meg. Meg's nostalgic exchange of childhood reminiscences with the visiting men emphasizes the childlike nature of all the characters and underlines their separateness from each other, a comment both on man's birth and his isolation.

Meg, who is incapable of recognizing evil, and hence incapable of helping,[13] joins Lulu and Petey as "the 'home folks' who stand by and watch Stanley undergo his torment."[14] Indeed, Meg's self-centered ignorance makes her oblivious to Stanley as the hunted or hunter, and she lingers the next day on her role at the party as "belle of the ball." The irony of the play, then, is based on the separateness of its strands, on Meg's awareness only of the surface rituals, the birthday party, the toasts, the games, rather than the brutal sacrifice which takes place before her very eyes and which she cannot see. Her unawareness only underlines the ritual counterpoint for the audience, who feel it more intensely in the frustrating light of her appalling blindness.

If the celebration of Stanley's birth progresses with all the weird logic of a nightmare, dream and ritual merge as the Hemingway-style killers move in on their prey. Richard Schechner writes:

> The famous antiphonal speeches of McCann and Goldberg are "tough guy" talk converted into ritual by abstracting words and phrases that in themselves have no direct connection to the play's action. . . . This litany continues for seventy-three lines. At the end of it, Stanley can no longer speak coherently.[15]

Edward Malpas, however, finds meaning in at least some of the seemingly senseless accusations of the tormentors. The climax of the interrogation reads:

McCANN: You betrayed our land.
GOLDBERG: You betray our breed.
McCANN: Who are you, Webber?
GOLDBERG: What makes you think you exist?
McCANN: You're dead.
GOLDBERG: You're dead. You can't live, you can't think, you can't love. You're dead. You're a plague gone bad. There's no juice in you. You're nothing but an odour! (P. 55)

Malpas suggests that "the crimes of which Stanley is accused mirror the subjective sufferings of the tormentors,"[16] the racial sufferings of Goldberg, and the national sufferings of McCann. Certainly the fact that Stanley is accused of every crime from picking his nose to killing his wife also suggests, in its tragi-comic way, the transfer of the sufferings and sins of the tribe onto a scapegoat. This role for Stanley has been foreshadowed by his story of being "carved up" in the past, and the psychological carving up within the scene is emphasized by McCann's ritual tearing of the newspaper, the shreds of which are all that is left of Stanley at the play's end.

Stanley's role as scapegoat clearly relates in some way to his defiance of the system and his betrayal of the organization. The play makes a bitterly ironic statement on the ritual sacrifice which merely rids the land of an ineffective nonconformist and allows the infusion through death of new life to a questionably brutal and empty system. Speaking of Stanley's fate, Franzblau writes:

> His fate is shaped at the hands of the representatives of the Establishment—Goldberg (the Jacob prototype), the man of words and platitudinous pseudo-reason; and McCann (the Esau prototype), the man of brute, servile force who begs for his blessing. They break Stanley's eyeglasses, robbing him of all clarity, and hurl a barrage of questions at him, challenging every consolation—from the sublime (religion: Do you recognize an external force, responsible for you, suffering for you . . . ?; or philosophy: Is the number 846 possible or necessary?) to the ridiculous (Why does the chicken cross the road?)—shattering every support. Stanley cannot attest his faith on any count. He has no escape from his cosmic perceptions or his resulting overwhelming depression. His insistence upon his integrity dooms him.[17]

Stanley, however, is not the only doomed person in the play. Although Goldberg and McCann verge on being stereotypes in the play—walking embodiments of the clichés they voice—the one-dimensional quality of their characters is not only disturbed by McCann's questions and obvious fear about the "job." The rich texture of Pinter's dialogue reveals Goldberg no less than McCann as partially a suffering victim.

Goldberg's false pose as a man of sentiment is hilariously set forth in his birthday toast.

> I believe in a good laugh, a day's fishing, a bit of gardening. I was very proud of my old greenhouse, made out of my own spit and faith. That's the sort of man I am. Not size but quality. A little Austin, tea in Fullers, a library book from Boots, and I'm satisfied. But just now, I say just now, the lady of the house said her piece and I for one am knocked over by the sentiments she expressed. Lucky is the man who's at the receiving end, that's what I say. (*Pause.*) How can I put it to you? We all wander on our tod through this world. It's a lonely pillow to kip on. Right! (P. 59)

Beneath the pose of the homey family man, however, Goldberg is not merely the man who Lulu complains taught her "things a girl shouldn't know before she's been married at least three times" (p. 84) and the brutal destroyer of Stanley. He is also the frightened and truly lonely victim of his own clichés who needs McCann to breath in his mouth to give him the strength to go on. In act 3, just before they take Stanley away, Goldberg reveals his uneasiness and finally his despair.

> GOLDBERG (*interrupting*): I don't know why, but I feel knocked out. I feel a bit . . . It's uncommon for me.
>
> .   .   .   .
>
> You know what? I've never lost a tooth. Not since the day I was born. Nothing's changed. (*He gets up.*) That's why I've reached my position, McCann. Because I've always been as fit as a fiddle. All my life I've said the same. Play up, play up, and play the game. Honour thy father and thy mother. All along the line. Follow the line, the line, McCann, and you can't go wrong. What do you think, I'm a self-made man? No! I sat where I was told to sit. I kept my eye on the ball. School? Don't talk to me about school. Top in all subjects. And for why? Because I'm telling you, I'm telling you, follow my line? Follow my mental? Learn

by heart. Never write down a thing. No. And don't go too
near the water. And you'll find—that what I say is true.
Because I believe that the world . . . (*Vacant.*). . . .
Because I believe that the world . . . (*Desperate.*). . . .
BECAUSE I BELIEVE THAT THE WORLD . . .
(*Lost.*). . . . (Pp. 79-80)

Here is T. S. Eliot's hollow man incarnate and the rhythms
of his wasteland as well.

McCann, the defrocked priest of six months, also vacil-
lates between refusing to go upstairs to get Stanley and
insisting that he never refused. The victors are the victims
of their own system, frightened in their moment of triumph
as any priest of Nemi might have been who conquered his
foe, but as modern in their malaise as any Beckett tramp—
and perhaps even more lost.

Meg's and Lulu's captivation by the agents of Stanley's
doom is part, too, of the structure of the dying-god ritual.
In such rituals the victorious god-king is almost inevitably
joined with a fertility goddess figure, even as Frazer believed the priest of Nemi was united with the goddess of
the grove whom he served.[18] Hence Meg flirts with the
visitors and plays the role of the queen at the party, "the
belle of the ball," and Lulu succumbs completely to the
spurious charms of Goldberg. No wonder Stanley attempts
to strangle Meg and rape Lulu at his party, during which
he battles for control. As the struggle for power is enacted
in the ritual celebration, Stanley naturally strikes out at
the deserting women.

That celebration is completed in *The Birthday Party*
when we are allowed to see not only the destruction of
Stanley but a glimpse of his resurrection as well, not only
the tearing asunder of the sacrifical god but the prospect
of what he will be when the pieces are put back together.
The two agents of "Monty" offer to fix Stanley's broken
glasses and broken life, to give him new vision, to save him,
to "renew" his "season ticket."

GOLDBERG: We'll take tuppence off your morning tea.

McCANN: We'll give you a discount on all inflammable goods.

GOLDBERG: We'll watch over you.

McCANN: Advise you.

GOLDBERG: Give you proper care and treatment.

McCANN: Let you use the club bar.

GOLDBERG: Keep a table reserved.

McCANN: Help you acknowledge the fast days.

GOLDBERG: Bake you cakes.

McCANN: Help you kneel on Kneeling days.

GOLDBERG: Give you a free pass.

McCANN: Take you for constitutionals.

GOLDBERG: Give you hot tips.

McCANN: We'll provide the skipping rope.

GOLDBERG: The vest and pants.

McCANN: The ointment.

GOLDBERG: The hot poultice. (P. 87)

Finally the men make clear the nature of the resurrection.

GOLDBERG: We'll make a man of you.

McCANN: And a woman.

GOLDBERG: You'll be re-orientated.

McCANN: You'll be rich.

GOLDBERG: You'll be adjusted.

McCANN: You'll be our pride and joy.

GOLDBERG: You'll be a mensch.

McCANN: You'll be a success.

GOLDBERG: You'll be integrated.

McCANN: You'll give orders.

GOLDBERG: You'll make decisions.

McCANN: You'll be a magnate.

GOLDBERG: A statesman.

McCANN: You'll own yachts.

GOLDBERG: Animals.

McCANN: Animals. (P. 88)

Stanley greets this incantation of his new nonidentity with inarticulate mumblings. Clean-shaven, newly outfitted in striped trousers, black jacket, white collar, and bowler, he is marched off to Monty utterly unable to see or speak, but with the promise of new vision, new speech, new power, new godhead—the latest remade model of conformity. As McCann repeats Goldberg's "animals," he underlines the animalistic destruction of Stanley's humanity which he and Goldberg perpetrate in the name of civilization. The use of ritual is satirical here as well as structural. The resurrection embodies all that is most superficial in modern civilization, all that is most precious to that civilization's corrupt emissaries, Goldberg and McCann.

Stanley's meaningless croakings tend also to belie the promised resurrection, and one is left with the sense of a stillborn birth or the creation of a manikin monster of nonidentity. The sacrificial rite at the center of the play does not leave its audience with that sense of renewal which gave mysterious pleasure to the audience at a Greek tragedy, but appears rather to parody those rituals which patterned tragic drama of old. The play stands, in part, as a bitterly comic comment on the ongoing cyclic nature of life, in which all that is most brutal and false in civilization is renewed at the expense of the most pathetic of rebels.

But Pinter does not rest in a merely comic or satirical vision. His play rather bears a strange resemblance to Eugene O'Neill's *The Iceman Cometh*, and O'Neill's attitude toward tragedy in that play also curiously antedates Pinter's own.

There is a feeling around, or I'm mistaken, of fate—Kismet, the negative fate; not in the Greek sense. . . . It's struck me as time goes on, how something funny, even farcical, can suddenly without any apparent reason, break up into something gloomy and tragic. . . . A sort of unfair *non sequitur*, as though events, as though life, were being manipulated just to confuse us. I think I'm aware of comedy more than I ever was before; a big kind of comedy that doesn't stay funny very long. I've made some use of it in *The Iceman.* The first act is hilarious comedy, *I think*, but then some people may not even laugh. At any rate, the comedy breaks up and the tragedy comes. . . .[19]

Pinter's statement about comedy several years later echoes O'Neill's, even as his play follows in the paths of its ritual rhythms and poetic insights.

Everything is funny: the great earnestness is funny; even tragedy is funny. And I think what I try to do in my plays is to get this recognizable reality of the absurdity of what we do and how we behave and how we speak. The point about tragedy is that it is *no longer funny*. It is funny and then it becomes no longer funny.[20]

This tragi-comic vision of both writers is manifested in the ritual counterpoint of the two dramas in which ritual birthday parties and cornflakes and rotgut rituals respectively are played out against sacrificial blood baths. Only the cowardly Petey in *The Birthday Party* and the equally craven drunken philosopher Larry in *The Iceman Cometh* share with the audience the full impact of the counterpoint.

The Birthday Party does not, then, remain a parody of ritual alone; its comedy moves into a realm which Pinter defines as "no longer funny." But the play's realm is not fully tragic either, and Pinter's tragi-comic vision may hold a clue to a more complete understanding of the particular use of ritual in his play.

The monstrous nature of birth in Pinter's play becomes more than comic largely because of the spark of resistance in the cowardly Stanley and the spark of awareness in the cowardly Petey. Stanley suffers, and his suffering and Petey's awareness give the play some of its tragic impact and ritual meaning. When Petey senses the menace to

Stanley, he attempts to prevent McCann and Goldberg from taking him away. However, Goldberg's insidious invitation to join them dismays Petey, who is left with his newspaper and the fact of Stanley's destruction in McCann's strips of paper, which fall to the floor as he seeks to resume his former self-protective reading ritual. The play then becomes an agonized protest as we share with Petey and Stanley the reality of its menace, the daytime reality of its nightmare.

It becomes less than a tragedy, however, as we seek in vain the heroic victim-victor of old whose defeat or death becomes less significant than the dignity and insight gained in the course of his suffering. For despite Stanley's actions on two levels in the play as both victim and victor, the total impact one receives places him still as victim.

On one level, Stanley appears in his *agon* with Goldberg and McCann as victor and victim—the hunted in a game of blind man's buff, but the hunter who attacks Meg and Lulu. Like the priest of Nemi, Stanley is no sooner born than he turns murderous. (Roger Pierce suggests that Stanley assists at his own birth when he attempts to strangle Meg and that his attempted rape of Lulu is a direct result of his new life.)[21] But unlike the priest-king, Stanley has not sought his role: rather, he is forced into life against his will. Hence, his victim-victor role in the *agon* still seems thrust upon him as victim.

Stanley's role as victim-victor on the play's other level emphasizes equally the victimized side of his character. At Monty's, as the carved-up god of old resurrected in new form, Stanley will become a puppet or manikin, not a man—and, hence, hardly a true god. Even Stanley as new god, then, projects the image of a victim. And the fact that Stanley's opponents in the *agon*, the battle between the old god and the new, are themselves frightened, potential victims of the god they serve, only emphasizes the total effect of man seen as victim in the play. The Golden Bough has lost its meaning for victim and victor alike; it is not worth guarding.

Myth, as Mircea Eliade defines it, reveals a reality of sacred time distinct from the reality of profane time. "In short," Eliade explains, "myths reveal that the world, man, and life have a supernatural origin and history, and that this history is significant, precious, and exemplary."[22] In his view, rituals allow one to participate in the deeper sacred reality of the myth.[23] But Goldberg, no less than Stanley in *The Birthday Party*, has a failure of belief in the sacred reality of the mythical line he has chosen to follow and which he is forcing Stanley to follow. The ritual is enacted with all its tragic implications, but the myth is called into question. Stanley has merely been projected as a new god by the god of old who still reigns. The ritual is a lie.

J. E. Frisch suggests that Pinter "directly questions" in his dramas "the usual concepts of reality. . . . He does this by working within a basically realistic frame of reference while simultaneously creating grave doubts about the reality of that frame of reference."[24] But Pinter doesn't question the reality of Monty's world, which dominates the play, so much as he questions its validity as mythical reality, as sacred or worthy of ritual renewal. Stanley's brief defiance of the cycle in which he is forced to participate is suggestive of another reality, of the possibility of a return to a Promethean defiance of a tyrant god, a life-giving myth, a reality from some other mythical time that lurks in the memory of man.

Nelvin Vos, studying some victim-victor relationships in *The Drama of Comedy*, describes the comic hero as one who accepts his own finiteness, and the tragic hero as one who struggles against the conditions of that finitude.[25] Like Eliade, Vos envisions time as either finite and profane or infinite and sacred. He suggests that the absurdist writers create victims who are "enmeshed neither in folly nor in moral imperfection but in finitude itself."[26] In Vos's opinion, for example, Ionesco's world looks mythical on the surface but is not.

> The circular plot structure of plays such as *The Bald Soprano* and *The Lesson* appears to indicate a mythic and ritualistic understanding of time and meaning, at least formally similar to that of Thornton Wilder. But, in Ionesco's theatre, cyclical time has lost all touch with a meaningful eternity and, instead, signifies a world of senseless anonymity and mechanism.[27]

Pinter's work, however, does not lack the interaction between the infinite and the finite which Vos suggests is needed for a true mythical structure and which Ionesco misses in the two plays indicated. Stanley's defiance does not place him in the realm of the victim-victors whose suffering reconciles them with the universe[28] and who assimilate death,[29] but it allows him a fleeting moment of awareness of something other than the world of Goldberg and McCann. He has had one concert in which he displayed his "unique touch," his one moment of self-expression and independence before he was locked out of the concert hall and locked out of life.

The play's texture is indeed complex. On one level occur the daily rituals—the paper, the tea, the cornflakes; on another, the birth and death of Stanley, the sacrifice and the resurrection, the initiation into Monty's world. On yet another level exist the questioning of the resurrection as valid, the denial of the validity of the cycle, the expectation and the awaiting of the new god. But in the meantime the wheel has turned.

The ritual sacrifice at the center of *The Dumb Waiter* is similar to that in *The Birthday Party*. McCann and Goldberg are seen at a closer angle in this one-act play, in which Pinter again on one level shows victim and victor as one and on another level portrays both victim and victor as victims.

In this farcical and terrifying drama two killers, Gus and Ben, await their victim and their orders in a windowless basement room. Again the ritual counterpoint operates as the killers' daily rituals are juxtaposed with the sacrificial rite which it is their office to perform. The manner in which Ben enacts the newspaper-reading ceremony, however, reveals his unawareness of the counterpoint. His shocked comments on the brutalities in the paper reveal his unawareness of his own brutality.

> BEN: Kaw.
>> *He picks up the paper.*
>> What about this? Listen to this:
>> *He refers to the paper.*
>> A man of eighty-seven wanted to cross the road. But there was a lot of traffic, see? He couldn't see how he was going to squeeze through. So he crawled under a lorry.
> GUS: He what?
> BEN: He crawled under a lorry. A stationary lorry.
> GUS: No?
> BEN: The lorry started and ran over him.
> GUS: Go on!
> BEN: That's what it says here.
> GUS: Get away.
> BEN: It's enough to make you want to puke, isn't it?
> GUS: Who advised him to do a thing like that?
> BEN: A man of eighty-seven crawling under a lorry!
> GUS: It's unbelievable.
> BEN: It's down here in black and white.
> GUS: Incredible.[30]

Ben has no inkling that his own activities in life are incredible, but Gus does have some awareness and concern about his own brutality. Tension mounts in the play as he begins to question Ben at length about the nature of the job.

> BEN: What are you sitting on my bed for?
>> *Gus sits.*

What's the matter with you? You're always asking me questions. What's the matter with you?

GUS: Nothing.

BEN: You never used to ask me so many damn questions. What's come over you?

GUS: No, I was just wondering.

BEN: Stop wondering. You've got a job to do. Why don't you just do it and shut up. (P. 99)

Ben meets Gus's further questions with more questions rather than answers, a pattern familiar from *The Birthday Party*, and the ritual framework of the operation begins to break down. Gus is concerned because the lavatory doesn't flush properly, because there is no wireless as in the last place, because Ben stopped on the road for no apparent reason, because the sheets do not seem clean. Even the tea ceremony is disturbed in this drama when the gas goes out, preventing the men from having their accustomed cup of tea before each "job."

The ritual counterpoint in *The Dumb Waiter* is handled with great dexterity, the tension mounting with the comedy as the naturalistic surface interacts with its ritual undercurrents. Gus and Ben's hilarious argument over an expression, Gus's "put on the kettle" (p. 97) as opposed to Ben's "light the kettle" (p. 97), would merely be amusing if the voice from the dumb waiter did not take sides. But his instructions to the men to "light the kettle" (p. 112) favor the unquestioning Ben over the questioning Gus— a foreshadowing of the final judgment that is passed in the play on Gus.

The comic *agon* between the two men is interrupted, then, by the written demands of the dumb waiter for exotic food, demands that neither Ben nor Gus is able to meet with satisfaction. Walter Kerr believes that Pinter achieves his effect of terror in this play, as in his others, because the terror is nameless, the hostile force not identified. The orders for food, Kerr notes, are explicit, but the orderer remains mysterious.

Was the building formerly a restaurant, and this the kitchen? Inside the basement flat, which is real, this sort of realistic speculation can be indulged. But it cannot continue to have meaning once it is applied to the world outside the flat: there can really be no restaurant which would send down orders to a "former" kitchen. Speculation is cut off in mid-breath, is plainly useless.[31]

Kerr further suggests that the inexplicable demands of the unidentified voice are at the center of the play despite their narrative irrelevance because they contribute to the undefined *angst* that modern man suffers.[32] In ritual terms, however, the intrusion of the voice's demands into the play's narrative is no intrusion, and the relationship of the men to its irrational presence and demands does more than spell out their undefined *angst*. Rather it tends to define the *angst*—to approach it with tragi-comic clarity.

Though the dumb waiter's instructions are not immediately connected with the job at hand, Ben later receives his orders not only for food but for action from the voice. As Malpas suggests, "The dumb waiter is no longer Bacchanalian, hungry for exotic dishes; this is Poseidon, primitively hungry for the flesh, the flesh of Gus the sacrificial victim."[33] And the victim is not chosen at random; the narrative moves directly toward a revelation of Gus as necessary scapegoat.

Not only has Gus felt uneasy about his job and surroundings, as well as the whole system; he has also dared to question the very god he serves. "Wilson" is neglecting their needs, he complains, and the dumb waiter is demanding more than is reasonable to expect. Beginning with something the men can comprehend, "two braised steak and chips. Two sago puddings. Two tea without sugar" (p. 103), its demands become more exotic: "macaroni Pastitsio. Ormitho Macarounada" (p. 108). Finally, they are incomprehensible to the men. "One Bamboo Shoots, Water chestnuts and Chicken. One Char Siu and Beansprouts" (p. 110).

Ben insists on being polite, but Gus yells up the tube; and when complaints come down about the nature of their substitute offerings—milk, biscuits, Eccles cake—Gus is openly rebellious. "We send him up all we've got and he's not satisfied. No, honest, it's enough to make the cat laugh. Why did you send him up all that stuff? (*Thoughtfully.*) Why did I send it up?" (p. 113).

Like Stanley, once Gus begins to question the system, he must be removed. His doom has been foreshadowed from the play's opening, so that when he notices Ben's slip in the final ritual rehearsal of their projected movements in removing the next victim—"I haven't taken my gun out, according to you" (p. 115)—clearly Ben as well as Gus has sensed the identity of the victim before the orders arrive. The questioner, the thoughtful gunman, one who has confessed discomfort that their last victim was a woman, one who is disturbed by the demands of a god for more than he is able to give, must die if the system is to continue. A repetition of the opening newspaper ritual takes place, but this time Ben does not reveal any content to which Gus may respond. Gus's automatic responses, delivered with the increasing despair indicated in the stage directions, are a dramatic confirmation of his defeat.

BEN: Kaw!
He picks up the paper and looks at it.
Listen to this!
Pause.
What about that, eh?
Pause.
Kaw!
Pause.
Have you ever heard such a thing?
GUS: (*dully.*) Go on!
BEN: It's true.
GUS: Get away.
BEN: It's down here in black and white.
GUS: (*very low.*) Is that a fact?
BEN: Can you imagine it.

GUS: It's unbelievable.
BEN: It's enough to make you want to puke, isn't it?
GUS: (*almost inaudible.*) Incredible. (P. 119)

Ben, who has unconsciously guessed that Gus is the victim, is nevertheless significantly surprised when it turns out to be him. When his partner stumbles through the door *"stripped of his jacket, waistcoat, tie, holster and revolver"* (p. 121), ready for the sacrifice, the two men stare at each other in "a long silence," and the curtain falls. The absence of a shot clarifies for the audience the nature of that silent moment of recognition for Ben. Ben too has been unable to satisfy the demands of the dumb waiter. Surely his turn will come. The killer must be killed. Victim and victor are one. "The light gleams an instant. . . . "

As in *The Birthday Party*, the victim-victors of *The Dumb Waiter* serve a god or a system which all of them fear and some of them doubt. This god, in the form of "Monty," "Wilson," and the voice of the dumb waiter, stands aside from the characters as a force that controls the closed world of the windowless basement in *The Dumb Waiter* and the seaside rooming house in *The Birthday Party*. Hence, the victim-victors in these two plays are felt to be victims of an outside force, a menacing god whom they serve or fail to serve at their peril, whose ritual renewal they are forced to enact. Stanley's attempt to escape the cycle and Gus's questioning of it remain, at best, pathetic acts of defiance.

Some further insight into the role of Pinter's heroes as victim-victors, who are victims of some exterior power, may be gained by looking at the playwright's adaptation of Adam Hall's novel *The Quiller Memorandum* into a film. In this 1966 film, directed by Michael Anderson, Pinter takes a good but fairly conventional thriller and transforms it into an enigmatic study of power. By turning an English spy with a personal vendetta into an American spy with no past or future that has any bearing on an extremely tense present, Pinter creates the script for a film that raises more questions than it answers and that leaves at least some of the "bad guys," totally defeated in the book, still very much at large.

The action of the book and film is set in West Berlin. Quiller is a secret agent assigned by the West to unmask the suspected leaders of a neo-Nazi organization or at least to discover their headquarters. (This identification of the "bad guys" as neo-Nazis was edited out of the film when shown in Germany by request of the German film industry's voluntary self-control organization.)[34] Quiller's new boss Pol, head of Berlin Control, informs him that he must find the headquarters without signaling British headquarters to the enemy. He is in the gap between two hostile enemies, and the film shows Pol, played by Alec Guinness, illustrating Quiller's position by manipulating cakes on a table. Pol eats a currant at the scene's end, very much as if he were eating Quiller, his own man. One can understand the appeal for Pinter in this isolated hero playing out his position in a gap, unable to trust anybody.

But if the gap of the isolated hero is closed at the book's end, it remains painfully open in the film. Rather than the Bond-like crushing of the entire organization by Hall's hero with an added achievement of personal revenge, Pinter's hero pays a final visit to a girl who will continue teaching her neo-Nazi doctrines to the school children who lovingly surround her. "We got all of them,"[35] Quiller tells the girl with whom he has fallen in love, knowing full well that she *is* one of them. "Well, not all of them, perhaps" (p. 14), he adds. When Inge tells Quiller that he looks tired, that he works too hard, he replies ironically in kind, "Well, you too. I'm sure you could take things a little easier, you know" (p. 16). But the film closes on Inge's assurance that she has her work to do and, indeed, wants to do it. Beneath the banal exchange lurks her defiance. Quiller has been cheated of both success and his girl. Pinter has characteristically refused a solution to the mystery; and his hero, at least in a figurative sense, is sacrificed—left on one level at least, in the threatened gap. A lesser work than *The Birthday Party* or *The Dumb Waiter, The Quiller Memorandum* is illuminating as a further exploration of man as the victim of forces which he cannot subdue, of man as victim even when he is victor.

3

Another Variation on the Theme of *The Golden Bough*:
Victim and Victor as One

"And what rough beast,
its hour come round at last,
slouches toward Bethlehem to be born?"[1]

The one-act drama *A Slight Ache* has much in common
with Pinter's other comedies of menace—*The Room, The
Birthday Party,* and *The Dumb Waiter.* Here too the
weasel from the first lurks under the cocktail cabinet and
emerges in a form both explicit and mysterious. The matchseller who haunts the back gate of Edward and Flora's
house in *A Slight Ache* is as concretely described, as realistically present, as the Negro visitor to Rose's room, the
Jewish and Irish agents of Monty who descend upon Meg's
boarding house, and the voice of the dumb waiter, which
makes its demands on the killers in their basement room.
Yet the reason for the matchseller's presence in *A Slight
Ache* is as mysterious as the appearance of the menacing
figures in Pinter's previous plays, and on one level his

identity is left equally obscure. We never learn in so many words who he is; certainly we do not learn it in his words, since the matchseller is silent throughout the play.

But the matchseller differs in several significant ways from the menacing figures in the earlier plays. He stands at the back gate of the house of a well-to-do couple—the lower-class victims of menace in the previous plays have given way to Edward, the country gentleman. The setting in which he moves is no longer a closed room; the action moves from breakfast room to scullery to study to garden, and the garden's presence on stage throughout is an important change of atmosphere from the closed-in settings of the other plays. Finally, the menace is portrayed as utterly passive in this play. Its demands are never stated. It is simply there.

The confrontation of ragged, stinking matchseller and elegant country gentleman has been interpreted on a social level by Augusta Walker, who sees the matchseller as a victim of the upper classes—"a spectre of his class, their [Flora and Edward's] discarded refuse, come to haunt them."[2] Edward's apologetic treatment of the matchseller and his comic attempts to bridge the social gap between them do indeed suggest a theme of social tension in the drama. And Malpas's point that Edward is drawn as a usurper whose working-class origins are disclosed in his confrontations with the stranger[3] contributes to a reading of the play in the light of class struggle. In such a reading the play would become a variation on the theme of *The Golden Bough*, the displacement of king-priest-god by a usurper who will in turn be displaced, in the modern idiom of social conflict.

The tension in Pinter's drama, however, moves on a metaphysical and poetic plane as well as on a social one. Far from a thesis or problem play, *A Slight Ache* incorporates whatever social problems it deals with into an exploration of the mystery of life and its renewal. Its setting reflects Edward's mind, "its openness representative of his mental vulnerability";[4] and Edward, as we discover through his interactions with the setting and his wife and the matchseller, is significantly different from Pinter's early victims, not merely in social station but in the more complex role he plays as the drama's victim-victor.

Whereas Stanley in *The Birthday Party* was seen as the dying god defeated in an *agon* with his tormentors but rising again in the new image they will manufacture for him, Edward in a far more complete way plays both roles in his *agon*. Stanley is to be remade in the image of Monty's desire; but as *A Slight Ache* progresses, Edward is identified with the matchseller who haunts him and who replaces him in his own home. In *A Slight Ache*, victim and victor are no longer victim—they are, in a sense, one and the same.

Esslin suggests that the play's radio audience (*A Slight Ache* was first performed on the BBC's Third Programme, on July 29, 1959) could never even verify the existence of the silent matchseller whose presence might be a mere projection of the couple and whose silence invests him "with the terror of the unknown."[5] Still, the matchseller appears on stage in the play's subsequent stage and television versions, and the drama is conceived as an *agon* between the two men. A ritual reading of the play suggests not that the matchseller is Edward's projection but that he is another aspect of Edward, who in one sense plays both roles.

Important clues to the double role that Edward plays in *A Slight Ache* and to the play's ritual meaning may be uncovered by exploring the double role played by the god Dionysus in Euripides' play *The Bacchae*. Here, no less than in *A Slight Ache*, the events of the play are more shocking than uplifting. The undefeated spirit of the tragic hero is missing as Pentheus, who denies the power of the god Dionysus, must pay for his blindness at the hands of the fierce Maenad followers of the god who are led by his own mother. Once in the power of Dionysus, Pentheus is paraded through the streets dressed as a woman and is reduced to a figure of ridicule: tragic recognition for this young man is limited to a pitiful plea to his frenzied mother for his life.

The more terrible recognition scene in the play is that of the mother, Agave, who later comes to see that the head she holds as her prize of the hunt is the head of her own murdered son. As William Arrowsmith suggests, this cruel scene shifts the balance of sympathy in the drama away from the triumphant god, who appears in the final epiphany as "a pitiless, daemonic, necessitous power."[6]

The Bacchae, however, may be less an indictment of the god[7] than an exploration of the ritual idea that god and victim are one, that the drama of Pentheus and Dionysus is the drama of the death of the old season and the birth of the new—the ritual expulsion of evil and the induction of good. Such a reading accounts in part for the particular nature of the tragic pleasure one feels in the play despite the unrelieved horror of its ending.

According to Northrop Frye, the sacrifice that is at the center of the ritual in *The Bacchae* is the very stuff of which tragedy is made. Sacrifice and tragedy, which is a mimesis of it, according to Frye, both share in a paradoxical sense of rightness and wrongness at the hero's fall. There is a sense of communion with the sacrificial victim, "the dividing of a heroic or divine body among a group which brings them into unity with, and as, that body,"[8] and a sense of wrongness, of need for propitiation, "the sense that in spite of the communion the body really belongs to another, a greater, and a potentially wrathful power."[9]

This double reaction, investigated at length by Freud in his *Totem and Taboo* in terms of the ambivalent feelings we all have for the primal father whom we would both destroy and become,[10] is evident in *The Bacchae*. Here Agave must pay for her union with the god with a full realization of horror at the act of killing her son and with exile. This paradoxical nature of sacrifice as curse and as blessing is clarified also in terms of the double role played by the god in the play. The play's myth, Hathorn suggests, reflects early customs of sacrificing human beings or kings "in the character of Dionysus."[11] The ritual base helps explain why Pentheus is tricked into going as willing victim; he is the seasonal god of fertility who is assured a rebirth. Agave becomes the destroyer as well as the preserver of her son in her role as fertility goddess: and the god appears in his epiphany at the end of the play only after his other self has been reborn, the body reassembled by Agave and the others.[12]

The above reading of *The Bacchae* has not satisfied all students of Greek tragedy, nor is it offered as a necessarily final interpretation of it. It has been, however, an important one lately for many, and becomes significant here because of the many parallels between the Greek drama and *A Slight Ache* and because of the light that a ritual reading of the Greek play may shed on a ritual reading of the modern one.

In both *The Bacchae* and *A Slight Ache*, then, a seasonal ritual may be seen to underlie the action, in which god and victim may be seen as one and the same. The opponents in the comic or tragic *agon*, the *alazon* and *eiron*, may be regarded as roles played by one god in different masks.

The *alazon* is an impostor, one who claims he knows more than he does; he is an enemy of the god, the *eiron*, who pretends that he knows less than he does. As previously noted, Frazer believed that the sacrifice of the old king became associated with the killing of a scapegoat (an *alazon*) upon whose head were "heaped the sins of the past year."[13] The *alazon* too could serve as a scapegoat "for the injury done the god during the fertility ritual."[14]

The god who is savior must be hated and slain. He has a double nature; he who is venerated, he who is reviled. Before the resurrection there is the crowning with thorns. The *alazon* is one of the disguises worn by the god-hero before he is sacrificed; he is also by the same token, the "antagonistic" self that must be disowned before the worshipper is "possessed" by the god.[15]

The sense of reconciliation evoked by *The Bacchae* is there, not because we exalt Dionysus as a necessary power over his weak victim, but because we sense the ritual beneath the events, the oneness of god and victim and the projection of both from the tribal group. Whether the mother-priestess presides over the death initiation of her son into manhood or over the death of the king–fertility god to initiate the new year, the cruelty of the sacrifice is mitigated by a suggestion of the new life to follow. And while the death of the old is emphasized, one senses the breaking down of tribal resistance to the god and all he stands for, a necessary event if the *alazon* and *eiron* are to be reconciled and give way to some figure in between, perhaps Aristotle's idea of the golden mean, neither *alazon* nor *eiron*.[16]

The compassion displayed by Agave, her father, and the chorus at the play's end, which Arrowsmith suggests makes them superior to the god,[17] is simply the refinding of humanity. And this humanity can be found only by allowing the animal side of man its province. Euripides becomes the humanitarian only by giving complete reign to the wonder and terror of that in man which projects the god Dionysus.

Stanley in *The Birthday Party* is in many respects a modern version of Pentheus as he refuses life's celebration. For him that celebration holds a forced death and initiation or resurrection. Stanley does not play the roles of both victim and victor in the play, however, since his roles are forced upon him by a truly malevolent power in whose image he is re-created. Edward, on the other hand, plays the role of *alazon* and *eiron* in *A Slight Ache*. He is subjected not to some outer force but to forces that lie within him.

The opening scene of *A Slight Ache*, in which the middle-aged Edward and Flora discuss the weather and their garden over breakfast, comically introduces Edward as god of the dying year and Flora as fertility goddess. Edward, hidden behind his newspaper during the couple's ritual interchange, reveals himself as ridiculously out of touch with his wife and his surroundings.

FLORA: Have you noticed the honeysuckle this morning?
EDWARD: The what?
FLORA: The honeysuckle.
EDWARD: Honeysuckle? Where?
FLORA: By the backgate, Edward.
EDWARD: Is that honeysuckle? I thought it was . . . convolvulus, or something.
FLORA: But you know it's honeysuckle.
EDWARD: I tell you I thought it was convolvulus.
   (*Pause.*)
FLORA: It's in wonderful flower.
EDWARD: I must look.
FLORA: The whole garden's in flower this morning. The clematis, the convolvulus. Everything. I was out at seven. I stood by the pool.
EDWARD: Did you say—that the convolvulus was in flower?
FLORA: Yes.
EDWARD: But good God, you just denied there was any.
FLORA: I was talking about the honeysuckle. (Pp. 9-10)

Superficially, the scene is merely amusing as it captures the small talk of people who are enacting a breakfast ritual. On one level the couple indulges in the "cross-talk" that Pinter believes people so often make in a "deliberate evasion of communication,"[18] but on another level the conversation displays a particular kind of withdrawal on Edward's part. When Flora insists that Edward knows perfectly well what grows in his garden and Edward insists that he does not, he is revealing very early in the play the nature of his blindness, the source of the "slight ache" in his eyes. Edward is out of touch with things that grow, with the examples of fertility in his own garden. He is out of touch too with Flora, whose name reflects the garden over which she presides as a kind of goddess. Thus Edward, in his comic way, is from the first a candidate for the role of the year god who must die, the old king of ancient ritual who represents the dying winter season and must be sacrificed to make way for the new.

Although Flora is depicted as an earth mother who will preside over the coming sacrifice, a comic and absurd tone mocks her role even as it is defined. Here is no maenad follower of Dionysus who sings, like the chorus in Euripides' *Bacchae*, of the wonders that flow from the fertility god:

> With milk the earth flows! It flows with wine!
> It runs with the nectar of bees![19]

Instead, a sense of clipped-off growth prevails. The names of the flowers, extravagantly sexual in connotation, sound ridiculous in the mouth of Flora, who produces a staccato rather than a flowing effect with her use of alliteration and her choppy sentences. "The whole garden's in flower this morning. The clematis, the convolvulus. Everything. I was out at seven. I stood by the pool" (p. 9).

Hence, while Pinter is setting the stage for the same kind of ritual drama that Francis Cornford suggests gave birth to ancient comedy and tragedy,[20] his rhythms are modern as well as ancient. Even as the tragic situation is set forth, the fertility goddess figure assumes a ridiculous shape; and comedy and tragedy mingle as they so often do in Pinter's dramatic world.

The tragic situation that develops as the play progresses is the sacrifice of Edward as scapegoat. As the play moves toward Edward's recognition of his identity with his opponent, however, Edward and the matchseller may be seen, on one level of the play's meaning, as two masks worn by the same person.

Initially, Edward describes the matchseller as an impostor, as the *alazon* who typically pretends to be what he is not and must be exposed by Edward the *eiron*, the one who knows more than he professes to know. Like Pentheus, who found the disguised Dionysus a charlatan, Edward identifies the matchseller as a fake.

> EDWARD: Damn. And do you know I've never seen him sell one box? Not a box. It's hardly surprising. He's on the wrong road. . . . Off everybody's route. . . . The whole thing's preposterous.
>
> FLORA: (*going over to him.*) I don't know why you're getting so excited about it. He's a quiet, harmless old man, going about his business. He's quite harmless.
>
> EDWARD: I didn't say he wasn't harmless. Of course he's harmless. How could he be other than harmless? (P. 16)

In this discussion, tension builds. The insistence that the matchseller is innocuous, combined with the idea of his being an impostor, suggests that he may well be harmful, that his presence at the gate for the last two months is not merely a nuisance but a menace.

As the menace grows, the matchseller himself appears to grow larger; he seems to Flora and Edward to take on the form of a bullock.

> FLORA: Good Lord, what's that? Is that a bullock let loose? No. It's the matchseller! My goodness, you can see him . . . through the hedge. He looks bigger. Have you been watching him? He looks . . . like a bullock. (P. 17)

Edward picks up the image of the bullock, the sacrificial animal or scapegoat, when his aching eyes push him toward the decision to confront the impostor.

> EDWARD: It's quite absurd, of course. I really can't tolerate anything so . . . absurd, right on my doorstep. . . . I

haven't wasted my time. I've hit, in fact, upon the truth. He's not a matchseller at all. . . . No, there is something very false about that man. I intend to get to the bottom of it. I'll soon get rid of him. He can go and ply his trade somewhere else. Instead of standing like a bullock . . . a bullock, outside my backgate. (Pp. 18-19)

Pentheus too comes to see the disguised god as a bull, a form in which the god of vegetation was frequently worshipped and sacrificed.

> PENTHEUS: I seem to see two suns blazing into the heavens. And now two Thebes, two cities, and each with seven gates. And you—you are a bull who walks before me there. Horns have sprouted from your head. Have you always been a beast? But now I see a bull.
>
> DIONYSUS: It is the god you see. Though hostile formerly, he now declares a truce and goes with us. You see what you could not when you were blind. (Pp. 195-96)

At the same time that Pentheus and Edward insist on the absurdity of the intruders into their lives and declare that they will get rid of them, their vision of them in the form of a bull is at the very least an intuition of the godhead of the adversary.

As Edward defines the matchseller as *alazon*—impostor and sacrificial animal—the tone of the play becomes somewhat sinister. The absurd is present, and the situation, as Edward suggests, is rather farcical; but Edward's fear is very real. The menace is invited in, and the "harmless" one brings with him a terrible reality. Edward is now revealed as the true impostor, the bullock who must be sacrificed. Just as the tables have been turned on Pentheus, whose efforts to shackle and jail Dionysus end only in the young king's own victimization, so Edward's attempt to ensnare his visitor ends in his own defeat.

The mute matchseller may indeed be part *alazon*, no matchseller at all. But he serves too as a peculiar instance of the *eiron*, accomplishing by his very silence what Socrates, the classical type of all *eirons*, accomplished by his questions and what Dionysus accomplished by his invitation to Pentheus to see the Maenad revels—the exposure of the *alazon*. Confronted with the silence of the matchseller, Edward is forced to look within himself, to confront the absurdity of his whole existence.

That absurdity is partly exposed as Edward tries to define himself to the matchseller.

> I write theological and philosophical essays . . . (*pause*) Now and again I jot down a few observations on certain tropical phenomena—not from the same standpoint, of course. (*silent pause*.) Yes, Africa, now. Africa's always been my happy hunting ground. (P. 23)

Edward's pretense of having "been around a bit" seems just as foolish as his expectation that the speechless and ragged matchseller standing before him has been around the world he describes. Soon Edward starts bragging, becoming more the buffoon as he goes; and when the series of clichés with which he describes his way of living meets with complete silence, he cannot help but hear their hollow sound himself.

> Oh, I understand you met my *wife*? Charming woman, don't you think? Plenty of grit there, too. Stood by me through thick and thin, that woman. In season and out of season. . . . Let me advise you. Get a good woman to stick by you. Never mind what the world says. Keep at it. Keep your shoulder to the wheel. It'll pay dividends. (P. 24)

When the clichés with which Edward has lived his life and which he now uses to protect himself from the matchseller fail to evoke a response, Edward becomes more and more frightened. Noting the matchseller's glass eye, a counterpart to his own aching eyes, he becomes exhausted and calls for air and for his wife. The account he then gives her of the matchseller is a good description of himself.

He's like jelly. A great bullockfat of jelly. He can't see straight. I think as a matter of fact he wears a glass eye. He's almost stone deaf . . . almost . . . not quite. He's very nearly dead on his feet. (P. 29)

Finally, half dead on his own feet, cut off from life, Edward confronts the matchseller a second time and admits the resemblance and kinship he has been fighting: "Why did I invite you into this room? . . . Well, why not, you might say. My oldest acquaintance. My nearest and dearest. My kith and kin" (p. 36).

The ensuing confusion about whether the matchseller is laughing at Edward or crying for him is important. Edward is, after all, both comic and tragic; the movement of the scenes exposes him as both to the audience and, through the matchseller's reactions, to himself. Overcome by his own insights and confused by the matchseller's reactions to him, Edward finally falls to the floor before the matchseller, who rises at Flora's command to take Edward's place.

When Flora presents her husband with the matchseller's box and role, the ritual sacrifice is complete. The *alazon* Edward has been exposed by the *eiron* matchseller. With Flora's aid, the old has been expelled and the new brought in. The sacrifice of tragedy is followed by the feast and marriage of comedy, in which the earth mother joins her new mate.

The fundamentally ritualistic structure of the play is reflected not only in the *agon* of the plot, but in many of the play's details as well. The references to weather, for example, which occupy a central part of the dialogue, underscore the movement of the seasons that is at the base of the ritual of the dying god.

The play opens at the height of summer, but for Edward, the dying god of winter, the weather is frightening. While his wife discourses on the beauties of the day, he informs her that the weather is "treacherous," and the weather becomes momentarily beautiful for Edward only after he kills the "first wasp of summer." The drowning of the wasp in the pot of marmalade, a comic version of the central sacrifice of the play, is surrounded by the usual cross-talk of husband and wife and carries a mock-heroic tone as Edward pours water down the spoon-hole of the marmalade pot. After the wasp is dead, Flora speaks of the "awful experience," but Edward suddenly speaks of the beautiful day.

Only Edward's perception of the presence of the matchseller at the back gate ends his rapture, and from that point the play moves steadily toward the sacrifice in which Edward is victim. In the wasp episode, however, Edward appears as both victim and victor. On one level the wasp symbolizes the matchseller, the arrival of summer, "the first wasp of summer," over which Edward triumphs. On another level, however, the wasp is a symbol of Edward as victim—another indication of the essential oneness of the two characters. Edward complains during the killing scene of the slight ache in his eyes, so that even in his moment of triumph his future role as victim is prefigured. Still, after the "murder" he does have a brief sense of renewed life, expressed in his recognition of the day's beauty. The incident serves as a flashback. The dying god was once the young god.

Indeed, Edward refers to the wasp incident at the play's ending with great nostalgia, treating the morning of the play's opening as if it were the morning of his life. Reflecting on his now ebbing strength, he says:

> I was polished. (*Nostalgic.*) I could stand on the hill and look through my telescope at the sea. And follow the path of the three-masted schooner, feeling fit, well aware of my sinews, their suppleness, my arms lifted holding my telescope, steady, easily, no trembling. My aim was perfect. I could pour hot water down the spoon-hole, yes. (P. 35)

All is in the past tense now, for even Edward begins to see that his role as the polished murderer of the wasp is ridiculous. "You're quite right, it is funny. I'll laugh with you!" (p. 36).

Edward's final speeches continue to reflect his concern for the weather and his role as the dying god of winter. He insists that he was able to cope with winter but describes a withdrawal to a womb-like state of passivity into which the menace of summer began to creep: "But then, the time came. I saw the wind. I saw the wind, swirling, and the dust at my backgate, lifting, and the long grass, scything together. . . . You're laughing at me! Aaaahhh!" (p. 39).

Here is the anguished cry of death, and at this instant Edward sees the elderly matchseller as young, recognizing his now youthful usurper as the young god. Now, too, Flora, who throughout the play has dwelt on summer at its height, announces that "summer is coming" (p. 40). As the matchseller rises to take Edward's place, the sense of seasonal change is emphasized by Flora.

There is no real contradiction in Flora's insistence during the play that summer is at its height and that it has just arrived. In her seduction scene with the matchseller, the restrained English matron emerges clearly as a sexual and motherly figure and gives the matchseller his rightful name.

> Hmmmn, you're a solid old boy, I must say. Not at all like jelly. All you need is a bath. A lovely lathery bath. And a good scrub. A lovely lathery scrub. (*Pause.*) Don't you? It will be a pleasure. (*She throws her arms around him.*) I'm going to keep you. I'm going to keep you, you dreadful chap, and call you Barnabas. Isn't it dark, Barnabas? Your eyes, your eyes, your great big eyes. (P. 32)

The day of Saint Barnabas, June eleventh in the old-style calendar, was the day of the summer solstice, and Barnaby-bright is the name for the longest day and the shortest night of the year. Flora merely recognizes her new god as the incarnation of summer itself, the advent of which is considered to take place at its height.

Though many seasonal fertility rituals were celebrated in spring, the opposition of winter to summer, which was also commonly celebrated, is more proper to the tone of Pinter's drama. E. O. James, in *Seasonal Feasts and Festivals*, notes that many such festivals were celebrated at the height of summer in order to preserve a sense of "renewal at a time of decline."[21] Hence, though Edward is rejected as the god of winter, and though Barnabas appears at the play's end as the "young god," reference is made to Barnabas's death as well. Flora says to him: "And I'll buy you pretty little things that will suit you. And little toys to play with on your deathbed. Why shouldn't you die happy?" (p. 33). The play, then, is hardly an unqualified hymn to spring.

Recognizing its undercurrent of ritual, then, clarifies the structure of *A Slight Ache* and helps to explain the nature of much of its content. Ronald Hayman cannot see the dramatic validity of the protracted wasp episode or of Edward's "slight ache,"[22] but both elements are clearly integral to the play's ritual meaning. The changing age of the matchseller, the changing time of summer, the changing attitudes toward the weather, all fall into place in terms of mythical logic which apprehends events, "not chronologically or sequentially, but as they cluster about some significant center of recurrent ritual."[23]

Although recognizing the ritual basis of the play and its counterpoint with the daily rituals of the couple helps clarify its structure and meaning, the manner in which Pinter uses the ritual gives the play its particular flavor and significance. Edward's uncertainty about himself and his position in life undoubtedly does have some of the social undertones some of its critics have pointed to. His death agonies may even reflect the lingering death of Edwardian England. An Edwardian of many hobbies and an expert in none, Edward's very announcement of his pain as a slight ache suggests in this interpretation a typically

British restraint as well as a typically modern inability to articulate today's prevalent malaise or anxiety.[24] Pinter too, on a broader basis, is surely depicting a modern crisis of identity in his portrayal of the alienated Edward.

Inarticulate as he is about his condition, Edward nonetheless gains a measure of self-knowledge in the course of the drama, his clichés giving way to a poetic expression of his insight. A *Slight Ache* takes much of its ritual rhythm from *The Bacchae*, but it is close also to the rhythms of *Oedipus Rex*. Man is no longer a mere victim of outer forces in this play; the menace is within. Like Oedipus, Edward would escape man's fate only to find that it lies within him. Oedipus, seeking the murderer of the king, found himself and suffered his own decree of banishment. So, too, Edward sought to rid his home of a menace. When he invited the menace in, confronting the matchseller in hopes of dispelling him for good, he too, in a sense, was faced with himself, and was himself banished from his home. Oedipus's growing insight, climaxed by physical blindness, also finds a counterpart in *A Slight Ache*, in which Edward's failing vision is accompanied by a growing insight about his own identity. Stanley was hiding from the menace without. Edward invited that menace in and faced it as himself. Gone are the grand gestures and articulate sufferings of Oedipus, but the rhythms linger faintly on.

Flora's role as a fertility goddess continues, though, on a more comic level. Agave, in Euripides' *Bacchae*, also plays the role of a fertility goddess, but she is given a moment of tragic recognition when she realizes she has killed her own son. Death as well as life takes on a terrible reality and full meaning in the Greek play. Flora's somewhat casual disposal of her husband and her vulgar embracing of Barnabas, on the other hand, tend to rob the ritual of tragic dignity. The horror of death as it is perceived by Edward remains, but life is envisaged rather as horrifying and ridiculous than as terrible and wonderful.

The absurdities of the play do not evoke laughter and tears so much as they prevent the full experience of either.

Perhaps the deepest irony of the play is its presentation of the *eiron* as a mute matchseller. True, his image gives the other characters a chance to project their own personalities (Edward sees him as jelly; Flora, as solid), but for the representative of summer to appear as ugly, stinking, and passive is as much a mockery of the life process as is the artificial garden in which the couple pretends to live. The images are the extremes of frigidity and bestiality, with Flora reigning as a tragi-comic queen.

In one sense, then, *A Slight Ache* looks back to the earlier comedies of menace. Edward and the matchseller, another aspect of himself, are not treated as heroic victors any more than Dionysus or Pentheus, another aspect of the god, are treated as heroic in *The Bacchae*. Edward's faltering belief in himself and his position in life has much in common with Stanley's timid sense of himself. And in a sense Edward is the victim of Flora, whose ongoing, life-giving force will always take on the new god—an indication too that the matchseller may well be her victim when the wheel turns again.

In another sense, though, Edward's position as victor-victim in this play takes on meanings absent from the earlier plays. In Pinter's tragi-comic vision, fertility itself is mocked, but a kind of renewal does take place in the drama. Curtiss M. Brooks, who has detected a similar mythical structure in *Waiting for Godot*, points out that in *Godot* spring never arrives.[25] No matter how ugly or comic the image in Pinter's play, on the other hand, life is renewed; no matter how ludicrous, the god of summer does arrive and receives an embrace, a welcome. He may not be the forceful, though cruel, god Dionysus; but he plays his role and Flora receives him.

Though Pinter mocks ritual renewal here as he did in *The Birthday Party*, the renewal in *A Slight Ache* is more valid; its rhythms more nearly approach a sense of ongoing life. Gone from this play is the outside force that dominates the action of *The Birthday Party* and *The Dumb Waiter.* No Monty, no Wilson appear—only the characters in the *agon.* Hence, Edward in his double role is truly victor as well as victim in the life cycle enacted; and no suggestion occurs that an outside force manipulates the cycle. Victim and victor are one in this play, in which the rhythms beneath the mockery are suggestive of celebration. The contention for the priesthood of Nemi is seen as cruel and absurd, but vital and alive nonetheless.

4

The Battle for Possession:
Defense of the Tree

Like most birds,
the robin sings only within his borders,
where he pours out his defense and defiance.[1]

"The Examination," a short story by Pinter published in
1959, describes a cyclic change of power not unlike the
action of Pinter's dramas. The narrator, who begins as the
examiner, ends as the examined; and it is hinted that the
exchange of power is continuous. The narrator was previously the examined, and Kullus was the examiner; the
narrator then took over as examiner, and at the end of the
story the wheel has turned once more.

The power struggle in the story remains mysterious and
abstract; the object of the examination and the content of
it are never specified. The narrator dwells, rather, on his
examination technique, one that involves particular arrangements of the room and intervals given him by Kullus.
These intervals are periods of silence that differ from

Kullus's other silences which form a part of the examination. "And so," the narrator explains, "the nature of our silence within the frame of our examination, and the nature of our silence outside the frame of our examination, were entirely opposed."[2]

While the nature of the examination is mysterious, the battle for dominance is defined by the silences; the narrator loses his dominance when he cannot follow Kullus's journey with understanding "from silence to silence" (p. 90). One is reminded of the defeat of Edward by the silent matchseller of *A Slight Ache* and of the fullness of silence in the frequent pauses of Pinter's dramatic world.

The struggle for control in "The Examination" is also defined significantly by the setting; the narrator is confident of his dominance because he has arranged the room, which is his. When they were in Kullus's room, the narrator explains, he was subject to Kullus's arrangement of window and curtain and, hence, subject to Kullus. Back in his own room, the tables are turned. "Yet I was naturally dominant, by virtue of my owning the room; he having entered through the door I now closed" (p. 91). When Kullus begins to dictate silences rather than accepting them as given intervals, the narrator begins to play the role of the examinee, a switch that again is reflected by change of place. "For we were now in Kullus' room" (p. 94).

The ritual transfer of power in Pinter's dramatic world almost always focuses on a room or a defined territory that must be protected or gained at all costs. Even as the priest of Nemi guards the tree and the Golden Bough knowing that his life is at stake, so the characters in Pinter's dramas battle for possession of place. "Two people in a room" Pinter once said, "—I am dealing a great deal of the time with this image of two people in a room. The curtain goes up on the stage, and I see it as a very potent question; What is going to happen to these two people in a room? Is someone going to open the door and come in?"[3]

Whether the living space in a Pinter drama is a place to hide (*The Room* and *The Birthday Party*) or a place to cling to with all the identification of self with room (*A Slight Ache*), it has all the ritual importance in Pinter's world of Frazer's Oak bearing the Golden Bough. Until the contender to the priesthood of Nemi plucked the Golden Bough from the tree, he was no threat to the reigning priest. Frazer's explanation for this aspect of the ritual is that the god of the sky may actually have dwelt in the reigning priest and dwelt in the Golden Bough as well. The priest-king may have "personated in flesh and blood" the god and guarded "with drawn sword the mystic bough which contained the god's life and his own."[4] The importance of Pinter's settings to the characters who dwell in them, the way in which these rooms become battlegrounds for possession, and their key place in the cyclic transfers of power that are often at the plays' centers is but further indication of the archetypal and ritual patterning of Pinter's dramatic world.

Robert Ardrey traces man's attitudes toward space even further back than his primitive beginnings. In his book *The Territorial Imperative*, Ardrey postulates an instinctive drive or inward compulsion "to defend an area of space"[5] as man's biological inheritance from the animal world. This compulsion for space is connected, in Ardrey's theory, with man's basic needs for identity, stimulation, and security.[6] Whether such an instinct for space is indeed our biological inheritance as Ardrey suggests, or whether our attitudes toward space are culturally determined, Pinter's plays seem to dramatize the "territorial imperative" as it works itself out in terms of man's deepest needs.[7]

In Pinter's dramatic world, then, setting works on many levels. It is nearly always realistically detailed, but its poetic undertones and ritual base lend it aspects of a symbolically mythical reality. Pinter's realistic characters move in these settings at once on the level of sheer animality, vivid embodiments of Ardrey's territorially compulsive man evolved from animal, as well as on the level of sacred mythical reality. Man is seen as both animal and god.

The battle for possession of place and for self-possession shifts its focus from play to play in Pinter's dramatic world. The playwright dwells on a young man's identity crisis in terms of his room in his radio play *The Dwarfs*; he shifts focus in *The Room* to a woman's fears of dispossession and her secret desire for it. He views the battle for possession in terms of a cyclic exchange of power in the television drama *The Basement*, in terms of the battle of the sexes in the television drama *Night School*, and in terms of a class war in the film *The Servant*. Focus is on the already dispossessed in the revue sketches; and Pinter's second major work, *The Caretaker*, is almost entirely worked out in terms of its setting and the battle for possession. The scapegoat figure still predominates in these radio, television, film, and stage plays, as Pinter explores victim-victor relationships; but the importance of the setting to the characters becomes paramount.

The need for space is clearly related to the need for identity in Pinter's drama *The Dwarfs* (1960), a radio play based on an unpublished autobiographical novel. The central character, a young man in his thirties, undergoes an identity crisis reminiscent of Edward's crisis in *A Slight Ache*, but more adolescent in nature. Edward's crisis meant total dispossession from his home, which reflected himself; Len's crisis is dramatized in terms of his wavering sense of place. Like a child trying to locate himself, Len dwells on elements in his room.

> There is my table. This is a table. There is my chair. There is my table. That is a bowl of fruit. There is my chair. There are my curtains. There is no wind. It is past night and before morning. There is the coal-scuttle. This is my room. This is a room. There is the wall-paper, on the walls. There are six walls. Eight walls. An octagon. This room is an octagon.[8]

Len battles for a sense of existence in an hour between times: "It is past night and before morning." He tries to put the fragments of the room together to form a shape even as he tries to integrate his fragmented self. "Look at your face in this mirror," he demands of his friend Mark, who is but another facet of himself. "Look. It's a farce. Where are your features? You haven't got any features. You couldn't call those features. What are you going to do about it, eh? What's the answer?" (p. 93).

Len clings to his room, to its elements, for security, but the room eludes him.

> This room moves. This room is moving. It has moved. It has reached . . . a dead halt. The light on my skull places me in a manacle. This is my fixture. There is no web. All's clear, and abundant. Perhaps a morning will arrive. If a morning arrives, it will not destroy my fixture, nor my luxury. If it is dark in the night or light, nothing obtrudes. I have my compartment. All is ordered, in its place, no error has been made. I am wedged. Here is my arrangement, and my kingdom. There are no voices. They make no hole in my side. (*Whispering.*) They make a hole, in my side. (*Silence.*) (P. 88)

The imagery of *The Dwarfs*, more a poem than a play, once more reveals the scapegoat figure trying desperately to assess and hold his kingdom. Pinter denies any specific reference to Christ in Len's "hole in the side,"[9] but the image is highly suggestive as Len's room becomes a kingdom and Len becomes the dying god-king who is later reborn.

> You're trying to buy and sell me. You think I'm a ventriloquist's dummy. You've got me pinned to the wall before I open my mouth. You've got a tab on me, you're buying me out of house and home, you're a calculating bastard. . . . Both of you bastards, you've made a hole in my side, I can't plug it! (*Pause.*) I've lost a kingdom. (P. 97)

The battle for possession of self, then, is enacted in *The Dwarfs* as a battle for possession of place, with Len's kingdom at stake. The images are reminiscent of T. S. Eliot's poetic world, with Len as a Prufrock figure who feels "pinned to the wall" or a hollow man who dwells among the dwarfs in their wasteland.

What are the dwarfs doing? They stumble in the gutters and produce their pocket watches. One with a face of chalk chucks the dregs of the daytime into a bin and seats himself on the lid. (P. 94)

The play also has Eliot's sense of salvation from the wasteland—though not in the poet's specific Christian terms—in Len's emergence from his ordeal with a feeling of new life. Recovering from his illness in the hospital, Len senses that the dwarfs are deserting him.

And this change. All about me the change. The yard as I know it is littered with scraps of cat's meat, pig bollocks, tin cans, bird brains, spare parts of all the little animals, a squelching squealing carpet, all the dwarfs' leavings spittled in the muck, worms stuck in the poisoned shit heaps, the alleys a whirlpool of piss, slime, blood, and fruit juice. Now all is bare. All is clean. All is scrubbed. There is a lawn. There is a shrub. There is a flower. (P. 108)

As the new flower emerges from the decay of the dwarfs' wasteland, Len is reborn. There are echoes of the dying king fertility ritual that patterns A Slight Ache and that concerns Eliot in his poetry; but here Pinter seems focused more on the ordeal of the young—the initiation ritual on which Eliade dwells, in which the young man undergoes a ceremonial death and is reborn into the mythically real world.[10] Len emerges from his ordeal with a new kingdom.

Perhaps because The Dwarfs is Pinter's most subjective play, the sense of place in it is largely described. In The Room (1957), his first play and one, unlike The Dwarfs, not tied to material from a novel, place functions in a far more dramatic way to enhance the meaning of the play's ritual action.

Rose, the central character, is unsure of her place, her room, just as Len is unsure of his room and himself in The Dwarfs. The room itself does not change as Len's room does, but all without the room is vague and uncertain.

"No, this room's all right for me. I mean, you know where you are. When it's cold, for instance" (p. 96), Rose assures her husband Bert. What lies out in the cold, however, and what lies outside the room in the very house she lives in are baffling questions to Rose. She wonders who lives in the basement with its damp walls (foreigners, perhaps), who lives in the house, how it is laid out, and whether it is full. A visit from the landlord only underlines her uncertainty, for Mr. Kidd, amusingly enough, has lost count of the number of floors and contradicts himself by informing Rose that the house is full shortly after telling her the upstairs people have gone.

The arrangements in the house become more, rather than less, mysterious as Mr. and Mrs. Sands arrive looking for the landlord, but not for Mr. Kidd. The couple assure Rose that it is as dark inside as out, that they have been in the yet darker basement, and that a man in the basement has told them that the vacant room in the house is the very one they have come to.

Rose's fear of dispossession is thus increased before the blind Negro emerges from the basement to summon her home. Her initial fear of the Negro and her defiance of him, followed by her acceptance and apparent recognition of him, do much to establish Riley as at least an emissary from Rose's father. One may read the subsequent fight between husband and Negro as a fight between husband and father.

> The woman receives the blind Negro as a father and her husband stamps him to death as a father-rival. The woman turns to the father, who calls her by her secret love name, because her husband does not speak to her at all and breaks his silence only to chant a love song to his truck.[11]

This psychological reading of the play is enhanced when we see Rose stricken with the Negro's blindness at the play's end. It is Bert, her husband, who has been the true enemy, not the feared stranger in the basement who is no stranger at all. The Negro, Riley, may even be Rose's own buried thoughts emerging from the depths of the house and her own unconscious mind, thoughts she has wished to avoid. Her husband's attack on Riley, then, is an attack on her own deepest wishes to desert him. Rose's fear of dispossession finally appears as a fear of her deepest desires, the wishes of Flora in *A Slight Ache* for a "new" old man.

The conclusion of *The Room* has been much criticized for its melodrama; the blind Negro is identified by Taylor as a possible left-over from "those gloomy Carné-Prevért films on which Pinter says he doted in his early twenties."[12] Although the *agon* between Bert and the black Riley at the play's end is rather abrupt and Pinter is undoubtedly a more subtle master of his craft in later dramas, *The Room* is still a completely coherent dramatic statement. As in Pinter's other early plays, *The Birthday Party* and *The Dumb Waiter*, the central character is viewed as victim. (In a later play, *The Homecoming*, Rose as Ruth succeeds in going home and becomes a more complex victim-victor; see chapter 5.) Torn between the pull of a silent, brutal husband whom she mothers and a call to return home as the child Sal, Rose is a victim of her own fears and of her husband.

The play is coherent, however, only when its seemingly incoherent setting is understood. The apparent contradictions and uncertainties about the house are obscure on a realistic level but clear on a psychological and ritual level. The house reflects Rose's mind; its uncertain outlines reflect her uncertain sense of identity even as Len's room eluded him with its movement in *The Dwarfs*. Its depths, the basement, send up the intrusion into her fixed life, her room; and she is dispossessed of her security, forced to face her deepest wishes just as Edward faces himself in the mute matchseller. Finally, it is Bert, not Rose, who will not allow intrusion; and the squabbling couple who visit Rose are a comic version of the larger battle between Rose and Bert. The contender for the priesthood is defeated, however, in *The Room*, and the Golden Bough is intact.

The contender for the priesthood is victorious in *The Basement* (1967), and here setting is emphasized even more than character; the play develops with the ritual rigor of "The Examination" as a cyclic change of place reveals a cyclic change of power. Stott and his girlfriend Jane take over Law's basement apartment in this television drama, but there is a suggestion that the apartment was once Stott's. The play develops as a battle between Law and Stott for possession, with seasonal and scenic changes reflecting the gradual ascendancy of the intruder. As the seasons move, Stott imposes his taste on the room, and Jane endeavors to seduce Law (there is some indication that she had once lived there alone with him). Law, however, denounces Jane to Stott. "She's a savage. A viper," he informs him, "she sullies this room."[13] A final fight between the men in a now barren room results in an apparent victory for Stott; the final tableau reveals Law and Jane outside the door of the apartment, endeavoring to intrude and begin the cycle again. The woman is clearly a source of competition between the men, but in this drama, at least, the woman goes to the loser of the major battle for place. She is not in any way first prize.

Woman is not first prize either in the television drama *Night School* (1960), in which the battle for possession of place occurs between a man and a woman. Wally, a young man who returns from prison, finds that his aunts have rented his room to a young lady. Both Wally and Sally allow their need for the room to interfere with their attraction to each other, and they indulge in identity pretenses that end in keeping them apart. Wally gets his room back, but it costs him Sally's love. One is reminded of Eugene O'Neill's *Desire Under the Elms*, in which the playwright suggests on a far more tragic level the destructive hunger for place as security that can rob man of love, pitting father against son, husband against wife, lover against lover.

Servant is pitted against master in Pinter's adaptation of Robin Maugham's novel *The Servant*, for a film directed by Joseph Losey (1963). In this film, the servant Barret manages to subjugate and corrupt his young master Tony until their roles are quite reversed and Barret is clearly the master both of his employer and, significantly, of his employer's house. "It is a film about possession; not merely who owns what, but who owns who."[14]

As in his other works, however, Pinter's sympathy (and Losey's as well) is with the victimized servant Barret[15] as much as with his victimized master. Pinter tends to see each character in the film playing a double role, master and servant, each man potentially a victim in the battle for possession, which the playwright envisions as part of the tragi-comic nature of life. Barret is portrayed, then, as understandably corrupt in a pervasively servile and corrupt world.

Losey has described Tony as "a young master who still lives in the Eighteenth century behind an Eighteenth-century facade,"[16] who cannot cope with the incursions of the twentieth century. Certainly, the house plays a visual role in the film which the screen's technique enhances.

> The house itself plays a leading part in the story: we first see it bare and dismal, then gradually it fills to become a cocoon of expensive, insulating comfort, then the pretentious good taste of its furnishings gets out of hand and there is a return to squalor—a crowded squalor, more repulsive than its original cold emptiness.[17]

The changes in the house mirror and effect the power struggle between the two men.

If *The Servant* still deals with the battle for possession of house and self, the poignancy of Pinter's revue sketches (1959), written after his comedies of menace and just before his second major work, *The Caretaker* (1960), rests very much on their characters' lack of place, their deterritorialized existence. In *The Black and White*, for example, two riders of all-night buses discuss their lack of any other place to go. "I wouldn't mind staying,"[18] the first old woman confides to the second, who shares soup and bread with her at a bus depot. The depot, it seems, will soon close down for its hour and a half "scrub-round," and its lonely inhabitants will be sent on their bus-riding way. Another woman's only place in life is at the head of a queue in the revue *Request Stop*, and the banal interchange between a barman and newspaperseller in a coffee stall in *Last To Go* suggests their lost sense of place and self.

MAN: I went to see if I could get hold of George.
BARMAN: Who?
MAN: George.
  Pause.
BARMAN: George who?
MAN: George . . . whatsisname.
BARMAN: Oh.
  Pause.
  Did you get hold of him?
MAN: No. No, I couldn't get hold of him. I couldn't locate him.
BARMAN: He's not about much now, is he?
  Pause.
MAN: When did you last see him then?
BARMAN: Oh, I haven't seen him for years.
MAN: No, nor me.
  Pause.
BARMAN: Used to suffer very bad from arthritis.
MAN: Arthritis?
BARMAN: Yes.
MAN: He never suffered from arthritis.
  Pause.
BARMAN: Suffered very bad.
  Pause.

MAN: Not when I knew him.
Pause.
BARMAN: I think he must have left the area.
Pause.
MAN: Yes, it was the "Evening News" was the last to go to-night.
BARMAN: Not always the last though, is it, though?[19]

"The last to go" is not only the last paper, but also George, who left the area, and the men who cling to trivialities on life's borders and in that sense have also gone. In a recording of *The Last To Go*[20] on which Pinter himself played the Barman, the pauses were extended, emphasizing the total isolation of the character and the terrible burden of living.

The revues are excellent sketches, moreover, for the profound study of the dispossessed tramp Davies of Pinter's second major play, *The Caretaker*. Pinter returns in *The Caretaker* to his native Hackney (the area is not designated in the play, but the house in the filmed version of the play is located in Pinter's old neighborhood). His depiction of his characters "at the extreme edge of their living," as he himself describes it, is reflected in their existence in an area "on the extreme edge of London."[21] Hackney is described by Donald Bryden as

a frontier where city and country gnaw each other ragged, the pattern of streets trailing off into weed and wasteland, the neon and billboard slogans signalling emptily over the Essex marshes . . . Hackney must be one of the few places in Britain where a cocktail cabinet might, just conceivably, shelter a weasel.[22]

The ritual struggle for possession and identity in *The Caretaker* is fought out, then, on Pinter's home territory and is informed too with his sympathetic and objective observations of the dispossessed of London's all-night haunts.

In this play, a homeless old man, Mac Davies, is taken in

by Aston, a young man who takes care of his brother Mick's house. Both brothers, Aston and Mick, separately engage Davies as the house's caretaker, a position from which he is ultimately dismissed by both. The play ends with a decree of banishment for Davies, a decree engineered partly by Mick, invited partly by Davies himself, but ultimately imposed by Aston.

The central irony of the play lies in the character of Davies. Unable to accept refuge from the generous and sympathetic Aston, Davies instead plays the role of usurper, tries to dominate the situation, trusts the wrong brother, and ends up exactly where he began, out in the cold. *The Caretaker* is a poignant portrayal of man's self-destructive nature, his seeming compulsion to live his life in the image of the cruel ritual of the priesthood of Nemi, a battle for possession and self, a sense of self as victim or victor rather than as one self among many. Father must defeat son (*The Birthday Party*), or son must defeat father (*The Caretaker*). They cannot live in harmony as Aston desires.

The battle for possession in *The Caretaker* is deeply explored, and the play gains power from the masterful and complex development of the three men, all evenly balanced "so that each is as real, as grotesque, as mystic, or as vaudevillian as the other."[23] And if many of Pinter's plays center on the theme of possession and dispossession of territory, *The Caretaker*'s characters are defined almost completely in relation to the house and their attitudes toward it.

Aston is "in charge" of the house; the play takes place in his room. He is the priest guarding the sacred tree, though at the outset of the play he is off his guard. The other rooms in the house, he explains to his invited guest, are "out of commission."[24] Those up the landing "need a lot of doing to," and those downstairs need "seeing to" (p. 12). The room itself is full of "stuff": boxes; various pieces of furniture—a gas stove that doesn't work, for example; a lawnmower, though the lawn is overgrown; a turned-over wooden chair; paint buckets; a bucket under a leak in the roof. The details of the collection reveal Aston as a dreamer, a collector of fragments that he is always attempting in vain to assemble. The furniture is there because "it might come in handy" (p. 16), and as the play opens we see Aston attempting to fix a broken plug that he is still working on when the play ends.

On one level, Aston's accumulated "stuff" resembles the smothering furniture of Ionesco's dramatic world. One is reminded, for example, of the hero of *The New Tenant*, who is buried in his own possessions. An exchange between Aston and Davies over the relative merits of different kinds of saws is as hilarious in its satire on man lost in the mechanics of the modern world as any of Ionesco's plays and is reminiscent of Pinter's revue sketch *Trouble in the Works*.

In this 1959 sketch, Mr. Wills informs his employer, Mr. Fibbs, of a workers' rebellion in his factory. It seems that they simply don't like the products, neither the "brass pet cock"[25] nor the "hemi unibal spherical rod end" (p. 92). They have come to hate "the straight flange pump connectors, and back nuts, and front nuts, and the bronzedraw off cock with handwheel and the bronzedraw off cock without handwheel" (p. 93). Thus in this delightful sketch Pinter mocks the importance of gadgetry to modern civilization.

The humor is similar, but the satire has tragic overtones in *The Caretaker*, as Aston sets out to buy his jig saw.

ASTON: I think I'll take a stroll down the road. A little . . . kind of shop. Man there'd got a jig saw the other day. I quite liked the look of it.
DAVIES: A jig saw, mate?
ASTON: Yes. Could be very useful.
DAVIES: Yes.
Slight pause.

What's that then, exactly, then?
Aston walks up to the window and looks out.
ASTON: A jig saw? Well, it comes from the same family as the fret saw. But it's an appliance, you see. You have to fix it on to a portable drill.
DAVIES: Ah, that's right. They're very handy.
ASTON: They are, yes.
Pause.
DAVIES: What about a hack-saw? (P. 25)

In the context of the play, Aston's desire for the saw that "speeds things up" (p. 26) is pathetic; it is clear that, despite his constant tinkering, he is far more the dreamer than the carpenter, a collector rather than a doer. Esslin sees him as typical modern man, seeking security and poetry in his puttering with gadgetry.

> In a world that is increasingly deprived of meaning, we seek refuge in being experts in some narrow field of irrelevant knowledge or expertise. In trying to become master of some electrical appliance, Aston is seeking to get a foothold in reality.[26]

What distinguishes Aston from most modern putterers about the house, however, is not only his lack of success but also his broader dream. His most prized possession is a Buddha statue. "What do you think of these Buddhas?" (p. 17), he asks Davies, almost as if he would inquire what the tramp thinks of him. For Aston is a visionary whose hallucinations, we find out later in the play, have led to his downfall. Aston's dream is not even centered primarily on fixing up the house he has charge of; he dreams rather of building anew, of building a shed in the garden.

At the end of the second act, we discover that Aston's dreams have been shattered before. Hospitalized because of his hallucinations and self-revelations (he willingly shared his visions with others), Aston tells of the operation in which something was done to his brain. A victim of society and of his own mother, whose permission was needed for the operation, Aston failed to make his escape—which, significantly, he attempted with a saw. "I spent five hours sawing at one of the bars on the window in this ward" (pp. 58-59), he explains to Davies.

Aston no longer talks to people, nor does he have his hallucinations. Instead, he collects the "bits and pieces" with which he hopes to redecorate the flat and build his shed. The jig saw which he set out to get had already been sold, and one recalls the failure of his attempt to saw his way to freedom.

But, if Aston cannot put the bits and pieces of himself or his projected shed together, neither does he allow himself to be victimized by his invited guest. He is, in fact, another of the victim-victor figures who populate the Pinter landscape. Having once been crucified by society, he is unwilling to be crucified again. His is a defensive position—unlike the priest of Nemi, he has no sword; he merely stands his ground. He will share his territory, but he will not give up his bed, or allow his window to be shut, or be bullied.

When Davies threatens Aston with another hospital experience ("They can put them pincers on your head again, man!" [p. 70]), and attacks his dream ("You build your stinking shed first!" [p. 72]), Aston gives the tramp notice that he must leave. "You stink," Aston informs Davies, not as an attack but as a fact. "For days. That's one reason I can't sleep" (p. 72). Once more, Aston has been open with somebody and has been betrayed; the play's action reflects his previous experience with society. This time, however, Aston holds his own. He still clings to his dream, undefeated. "That's not a stinking shed," he assures Davies. "It's clean. It's all good wood. I'll get it up. No trouble" (p. 72).

Aston, then, is a dreamer who invites Davies to share his domain and evicts him when he sees the tramp's incapacity to share. Aston's brother Mick, on the other hand, is a man of action who considers Davies an intruder on what is his domain. Whereas Aston is direct and open with Davies, Mick is indirect and possessive. He seems to enjoy the invasion of his property, his room, his bed, much as Robert Ardrey suggests man and animal gain stimulation and identity from border skirmishes or territorial challenges.[27] He enjoys tormenting the old man, accusing him of smelling one minute, flattering him by asking his advice another, accusing him of trespassing only to offer him the position of caretaker that his brother has already offered him.

Mick's sadistic behavior has challenged critics, who have given him the role of devil to Aston's Christ,[28] or of fellow conspirator with Aston in Davies's ruin.[29] Terrence Rattigan has even designated Mick as the Old Testament God, with Aston the New Testament God and Davies Humanity, an interpretation that caused Pinter to reply "that the play was about a caretaker and two brothers."[30]

The realistic complexity of the play does undermine an oversimplified allegorical interpretation. Lloyd Busch has suggested the weakness in Schechner's interpretation of Aston as even a passive conspirator in Davies's defeat by pointing out that Aston is "generous and long-suffering to a fault,"[31] and the complex relationship of the two brothers calls into question an interpretation that would make them either opposites (devil and god) or conspirators. In this basically territorial play, important clues to Mick's motivation and his character lie, however, in Mick's attitude toward the house.

Mick, like Aston, is a dreamer; but his dreams for the house differ from his brother's dreams. He is a man on the move, an owner of a van, a member of the building trade. While Aston dreams of his simple, clean shed, Mick dreams of a penthouse palace.

> I could turn this place into a penthouse. For instance . . . this room. This room you could have as the kitchen. Right size, nice window, sun comes in. I'd have . . . I'd have teal-

82

blue, copper and parchment linoleum squares. I'd have those colours re-echoed in the walls. I'd offset the kitchen units with charcoal-grey worktops. Plenty of room for cupboards for the crockery. We'd have a small wall cupboard, a large wall cupboard, a corner wall cupboard with revolving shelves. You wouldn't be short of cupboards. You could put the dining-room across the landing, see? Yes. Venetian blinds, venetian blinds on the window, cork floor, cork tiles. You could have an off-white pile linen rug, a table in . . . in afronomosia teak veneer, sideboard with matt black drawers, curved chairs with cushioned seats, armchairs in oatmeal tweed, . . . it wouldn't be a flat it'd be a palace. (Pp. 63-64)

The central conflict in the play actually occurs between the brothers, between whom Davies moves as a catalyst, inadvertently collecting their dreams. Aston's collection of odds and ends is "junk" in Mick's eyes, for Mick's imagination moves in the modern vein, soaring to penthouse heights, whereas Aston is a carpenter and man of the soil who would build with good clean wood. Mick complains to Davies that Aston isn't interested in his plans. In fact, Aston doesn't like work, Mick confides. "Causing me great anxiety. You see, I'm a working man, I'm a tradesman," he explains. "I've got my own van" (p. 51).

Aston is causing his brother anxiety, but not simply because he won't work. Aston is taking care of Mick's house, but Mick is clearly his brother's keeper. Who will live in the projected palace of Mick's dream, Davies inquires. "I would, my brother and me" (p. 64), Mick replies, pointedly leaving the tramp out. The tramp, indeed, is only included by Mick, hired by him as caretaker, because he wishes to communicate with Aston and finds it hard to do so directly.

The ambivalence of Mick's feelings for his brother is revealed in several ways. Their first direct interchange is a conversation over the leaking roof; Mick asks about it, and Aston says he will fix it. Mick is impatient but not openly critical. He does challenge Aston indirectly, however, when he takes the bag of clothes which Aston has brought for Davies and which the three men fight over in a kind of music-hall pantomime routine. After a final series of grabs for the bag by each man, Aston gives it to Mick, who gives it to Davies. Mick will not defy his brother's trust in him. The brothers do manage an effective, if silent, communication through their gestures.

Mick further shows his mixed feelings toward his brother in the way he attacks Aston verbally to Davies and then jumps on Davies whenever he agrees or takes the criticism farther. In fact, Lloyd Busch believes that Mick's hostile treatment of the old tramp is a means of expressing hostility toward Aston, who hampers his progress and at whom he strikes more directly when he breaks Aston's beloved Buddha. He is restrained from a more direct attack on Davies, Busch believes, because of some ties of affection for his brother and concern for his illness.[32]

Perhaps Busch underestimates those ties of affection when he sees Mick's motives as masked hostility toward his brother. Mick's interest in Davies, whom he sees through from the first, is an extension of his interest in his brother, who infuriates him and whom he loves. Thus he traps Davies rather than throwing him out, engineering matters so that his brother will see Davies for what he is, an intruder. The climax of the play, Mick's smashing of his brother's most prized possession, his Buddha, is not an expression of Mick's hostility but an expression of his effort to free himself from his brother, to whom he has felt strongly tied. After dismissing Davies and smashing the Buddha, Mick speaks to himself broodingly:

Anyone would think this house was all I got to worry about. I got plenty of other things I can worry about. I've got other things. I've got plenty of other interests. I've got my own business to build up, haven't I? I got to think about expanding . . . in all directions. I don't stand still. I'm moving about, all the time. I've got to think about the future. I'm not worried about this house. I'm not interested. My brother can worry about it. He can do it up, he can decorate it, he can do what he likes with it. I'm not bothered. I thought I was doing him a favour, letting him live here. He's got his own ideas. Let him have them. I'm going to chuck it in. (P. 78)

The tone is that of over-protest—Mick is still interested, bothered. But he will "chuck" the house and let his brother have it to do with it as he likes. He will move on—follow his own path. Hence, Mick's smashing of the statue releases his feelings of impatience not only with his brother but also with himself. When the brothers meet, they exchange smiles of understanding. Aston is not overly disturbed by the broken statue. The tramp has been banished, and Mick has at last accepted Aston for what he is. He realizes Aston cannot inhabit *his* dream and accepts the situation he has fought so deeply.

In his own way, Mick is as dispossessed as Davies is. His ironically sadistic taunting of Davies about his identity (he badgers him about his name, his references, his bank account) reflects an unsureness about his own identity. When he finally unmasks the old man as "a bloody impostor," a "wild animal," the "barbarian," identifying him as the play's *alazon*-scapegoat who must be banished, one is reminded of Edward's confrontation with the matchseller in A *Slight Ache*. Mick is on surer ground than Edward. He is young, alive, on the move, not ready as yet to see the "wild animal" or "barbarian" in himself—witness his barbaric treatment of the old man. But Mick's decision to move on and leave his brother the house places him in a world as unsure as that of Davies.

Mick's irony is directed against himself as much as it is directed against Davies. His tone suggests self-doubt even about his decorator's vision. "You're the only man I've told about my dreams," Mick taunts Davies, "about my deepest wishes . . . and I only told you because I understood you were an experienced first-class professional interior and exterior decorator" (p. 76). Davies cannot fathom Mick's language, nor deliver the goods. "You mean you wouldn't know how to fit teal-blue, copper and parchment linoleum squares and have those colours re-echoed in the walls?" (p. 76), Mick asks him with cruelty; but the ironical tone betrays self-doubt in the dream itself. Can he possess his own dream? Is it inhabitable?

If Mick is the catalyst, then, who speeds the expulsion of Davies from his newfound haven, Davies is the catalyst who speeds Mick's own removal from that haven. Mick's machinations with the old man take on a "devilish" aspect only insofar as he shares with his victim that ultimate sense of dispossession with which he taunts him.

Davies, however, is far more his own victim than he is that of Mick. Literally incapable of accepting hospitality, he is prevented by his own shaken sense of identity (his papers are in Sidcup, and he is unable to get himself to pursue them) from accepting the offered haven on a sharing basis. His self-imposed role as victim is built on a deep distrust of himself and of others. Everybody is always letting him down. His own shoes will not serve him, but he cannot accept those Aston offers. He cannot drink Guinness from a thick mug, only a thin glass. He cannot be comfortable in a bed when there is a draft from an open window. A checked shirt will never serve him in the winter. "No, what I need, is a kind of a shirt with stripes, a good solid shirt, with stripes going down" (p. 43).

Unwilling to work for his keep, uncomfortable that the "blacks" on the street may invade, Davies has all the prejudices of the insecure, all the fears of eviction that lead him to attempt to play the brothers off against each other so that he may rule. The one gift he is able to accept from Aston is, amusingly enough, a smoking jacket, a gift that supplies him with the image he desires, that of the leisured proprietor of his own domain.

When Esslin suggests that Davies's expulsion from the

house "assumes almost the cosmic proportions of Adam's expulsion from Paradise,"[33] he is not reducing the play to allegory but suggesting the universal nature of this very particular old man's predicament. "Davies' lying, his assertiveness, his inability to resist any chance to impose himself as superior, are, after all, mankind's original sin—hubris, lack of humility, blindness to our own faults."[34]

Davies, no less than Mick, has his moment of recognition at the play's end. He has put his trust in the wrong brother, and he knows it. "What am I going to do?" (p. 81), he asks pathetically; and, despite his guilt and his unattractive behavior, his situation draws sympathy. "The final image is achieved," writes Richard Gilman, "of unbearable loneliness, of war in the members of the body, and yet also of persistent blind movement toward communion and authentic life."[35] Far from a plotless play, The Caretaker's structure is built upon that war in the members and ends in more than despair as the trio "go on finding themselves through what they cannot find in others."[36]

In some ways, The Caretaker is another comedy of menace as Mick terrifies the tramp with a vacuum cleaner in the dark, and Davies threatens each brother with a knife. Pinter's choice of a nonviolent ending for the play, which he originally planned to end with Davies's death, places the play, however, more in the vein of A Slight Ache, in which the source of menace is as much within as without. The Monty and Wilson of The Birthday Party and The Dumb Waiter linger on in the image of the operation Aston underwent, but Mick and Davies are victimized mainly by themselves.

In some respects, the three characters in The Caretaker are all dispossessed, all in search of their identity papers in a materialistic world that each seeks to shape to his dreams and in which each feels lost. In The Dwarfs, Len's search for his identity centered largely on his sense of place; and the search was subjective and thoroughly described. In *The Caretaker*, Pinter achieves a masterpiece of drama by his full and objective development of three characters whose interactions with a room and with each other offer a darkly comic and poignant reading of man's fragmented life in modern society. Aston's attempt at the play's end to fix the plug that he was working on at its beginning is suggestive of a continued attempt to make a connection, despite his failure to connect with Davies. His activity assumes the nature of a ritual attempt to repair, a ritual in which Mick no longer believes, but Aston does. Mick has protected the wounded priest of Nemi from an intruding contender and has left him with his fragmented Golden Bough.

The ritual battle for possession of place in *The Caretaker* is beautifully captured in the 1963 film version of the play as directed by Clive Donner. This low budget (£30,000), prize-winning film (the film was awarded a Silver Bear at the Berlin Film Festival for its production, direction, script, and acting) was a unique venture in film-making. Conventional sources of film finance were withdrawn; and Pinter, the producer, Michael Burkett, and the actors, Donald Pleasence, Alan Bates, and Robert Shaw formed a special company in order to make the film. This arrangement allowed them to work closely and freely in what was totally their own venture. Donner describes with enthusiasm an initial eleven-hour meeting of the company on the transfer of the play to the screen, the three-week rehearsal period before shooting—a somewhat unusual feature of his film direction—and a last-day five-hour rehearsal of the whole piece with Pinter present.[37] Filmed on location at a house in Hackney not far from Pinter's birthplace, with Donald Pleasence and Alan Bates re-creating their stage roles of the tramp Davies and the brother Mick, the film was the culmination and fruition of a long stage-run as well as an intensive film rehearsal period.

The transfer of the play to the screen enabled Pinter to

make an important point about the entire body of his
work: he invisions his characters realistically living in
actual places, not operating symbolically in a void. Pinter's
feeling that the core of our lives is ambiguous and nonverifiable has often become confused with an attempt to
mystify his audience about the background of his characters. In the film version of *The Caretaker*, Mick appears in
his van; there is a garden outside, a café at the corner.
Pinter found particular satisfaction in clearing up this
"real" background for his characters in *The Caretaker*;[38]
and his films, by the very nature of the medium, tend to
accentuate the naturalistic surface which he so lovingly
creates in his dramatic world.

If the filming of *The Caretaker* on location emphasized
the "reality" of the claustrophobic attic room, the additional outside scenes underlined the need of the tramp for the
room and helped to clarify the relationship of the brothers
to the house and to each other. The cold, snowy scenes outside dramatized the tramp's need for a home, making his
inevitable expulsion more pathetic; and Donner requested
an addition from Pinter, a remark on the snow by Davies.
"What about all this bastard snow now? I mean . . . when
is it going to go?"[39] Davies complains, a marvelously char-
acteristic remark for the tramp, the eternal victim in his
own eyes, even of the weather. A scene in which Mick
offers Davies a ride to Sidcup in his van not only emphasizes the reality of Mick's life outside, as well as inside, the
room, but emphasizes as well the suffering of Davies, who
might have to make good his boasting of locating his
papers and identity in Sidcup. It emphasizes too the
macabre humor of the taunting Mick, who deposits the
tramp back where he picked him up after a short ride
around the block and some feeble excuses. Pinter also
added a silent scene of communication between the brothers. "The brothers," Donner explained in an interview, "do
not speak, Mick staring into the pond, Aston at some wood

and then the pond. Davies is at the window wondering what they are looking at." Here Donner touched his nose in the manner of Davies. "Nosey,"[40] he explained.

The film then, faithful to the play, actually clarified some of the nature of the character relationships and conflict through careful use of image in moments of silence, through careful use of sound (the film opened with a dripping sound, ominous in the surrounding silence), through the additional "van" scene with its emphasis on the rather brutal humor of the piece,[41] and through the concentration on the weather, which added a dimension both to the play's realism and to its ritual base.[42] Pinter, in fact, admired Donner's work on the film, not only because it cleared up unwanted ambiguities in the drama's realism, but because inside and outside Donner concentrated on the characters "almost as if only these characters exist."[43] Hence this masterful film succeeded not only in capturing the very realistic texture of Pinter's dramatic world but also the intensity of his characters who operate as if they alone make up the world. The characters in the film are at once unique, real individuals living in a real world and archetypal figures who engage in a ritual battle for possession which is at the center of Pinter's vision of the world.

The Fertility Goddess
And the Riddle of the Sphinx

"As to your mother's marriage bed,—don't fear it.
Before this, in dreams too, as well as oracles,
Many a man has lain with his own mother."[1]—Jocasta in
Sophocles' *Oedipus the King.*

When Oedipus solved the riddle of the Sphinx, his confident solution was "man." The half-woman, half-beast left
him with a larger riddle, however, the riddle of himself as
man. Jocasta gave him a clue to its solution when she told
him that it was not an uncommon dream of man to lie
with his own mother. This dream haunts Pinter's dramatic
world. As Pinter explores the riddling nature of man in his
drama, at the heart of the riddle is man's ambivalent relationship with woman.

The only women in *The Caretaker* are the ones men-
tioned by Aston and Davies. Aston is puzzled by the advances made to him by a woman he merely chatted with in
a café, a common occurrence, Davies assures him, in his
own experience. Davies also speaks with disgust of his

wife, whom he left when he found her unwashed under-clothing in a vegetable pan. In *A Slight Ache*, Edward calls his model, middle-class wife a "lying slut," an appellation perhaps justified later when Flora embraces the stranger at their door as her new mate. In *The Collection*, Stella informs her husband of a passing affair and tantalizes him as the play proceeds with the question of its existence in reality or in her fantasy. And in *The Homecoming*, Ruth sends her respectable professor husband back to their three children in America while she remains with his all-male family in England in the combined role of mother, wife, and whore.

In Pinter's dramatic world, women continually play the double role of Sarah in *The Lover*, the role of wife and mistress as she envisions it or the role of wife and whore as her husband Richard comes to see it. The male reaction to women bristles with ambivalence and Oedipal tension as men struggle to keep their love for their wives and their lust for their whores separate (*Tea Party*) or to bring them together (*The Lover*). Martin Esslin sees this Oedi-pal tension developing through Pinter's three major plays with Stanley deprived of his mother (Meg) by his father (Goldberg and McCann) in *The Birthday Party*, the two brothers evicting their father in *The Caretaker*, and the sons realizing their dream of possessing the mother in *The Homecoming*.[2]

Such psychological speculation about the male-female relationships in Pinter's drama is most fruitful, however, if seen in perspective with the complex texture of the plays and their ritual base. Pinter's plays are most definitely not case histories. No matter how bizarre or shocking Sarah's behavior in *The Lover* or Ruth's behavior in *The Home-coming* seems on the surface, it makes a good deal of sense vis-à-vis the poetic and ritual nature of the works. As Pinter himself remarked with impatience, after reading Dr. Franzblau's reduction of *The Homecoming* to a question of homosexuality, "It's about love and lack of love. The people are harsh and cruel to be sure. Still they aren't acting arbitrarily but for very deep-seated reasons."[3] To reduce such a complex investigation of love and family relationships to a homosexual explanation is as limited as to read *Hamlet* only as a tale of an Oedipus complex,[4] or to reduce Sophocles' *Oedipus Rex* to its component of psychological aberration.

Still, Freud's attempt to investigate the psychology of Frazer's findings in his book *Totem and Taboo* is relevant to an understanding of Pinter's work. Although the book is an investigation of similar behavior between the neurotic and the savage, it does not focus on ritual as aberration so much as it attempts to gain a deeper understanding of the patterns of behavior that move all men. Pinter's drama too, despite his brilliant depiction of individuals, becomes at its best an exploration of patterns that we all inherit and share.

Freud, who found the basis of all neurosis in the Oedipus complex, concludes in *Totem and Taboo* that "the beginnings of religion, ethics, society, and art meet in the Oedipus complex."[5] In the light of his conclusions, it is not surprising to find Oedipal conflict at the center of Pinter's ritual dramas. The ambivalent attitude of the savage to his king is likened by Freud to the ambivalent attitude of the child to his father. The fertility rituals that Frazer explores and Pinter employs are examined as part of the competition of father and son for the mother. Witness his discussion of the death and rebirth of the vegetation god, whom he envisions as the son laboring over mother earth, youthful figures like Attis, Adonis, and others "who enjoyed the favours of maternal deities and committed incest with the mother in defiance of the father."[6] In mythology, Freud expounds, these deities are visited with short life or castration as punishment for their deeds; and their punishment is often visited upon them by their wrathful fathers, who appear in animal form.[7]

The rituals investigated by Frazer are open to varied

psychological interpretation and take on different meanings in later anthropological studies. Gilbert Murray in "Hamlet and Orestes" discusses "the world-wide ritual story of what we may call the Golden Bough kings" as it "forms the basis of Greek tragedy"[8] and is incorporated into Shakespeare's *Hamlet*. As well as giving two basic alternatives for the seasonal ritual—one in which the summer vegetation spirit is slain by Winter and rises in the spring, the other in which the year-king slays the old king, weds the queen, grows proud, and is slain by the avenger of the former king[9]—Murray presents various alternatives for the role of the female in the ritual. The queen might marry her husband's slayer (Gertrude, Jocasta) or be slain with him (Clytemnestra). She might help the usurping son, or even marry him (Jocasta),[10] though Jocasta as well as Gertrude and Clytemnestra die with their usurping second husbands.

Murray notes that in literature the queen mother or earth mother is often treated with sympathy, whatever incestuous, adulterous, or murderous paths she follows.[11] Moral disapproval may be suspended, he suggests, when the vegetation ritual is seen to be at the basis of some of the incestuous or murderous acts, though such myths harbor the seeds of moral conflict.

> But later on, when life has become more self-conscious and sensitive, if once a poet or dramatist gets to thinking of the story, and tries to realize the position and feelings of this eternally traitorous wife, this eternally fostering and protecting mother, he cannot but feel in her that element of inward conflict which is the seed of great drama. She is torn between husband, lover, and son. . . .[12]

Pinter's own treatment of "the eternally traitorous wife" is often deeply sympathetic, although the focus in his plays varies, sometimes lighting on the suffering husband (Edward in *A Slight Ache*, Disson in *Tea Party*), sometimes on the suffering son (Stanley in *The Birthday Party*), and sometimes on the suffering woman (Rose in *The Room*, Stella in *The Collection*, Ruth in *The Homecoming*). His treatment of the sexual relationship is usually ritualized, however; thus, despite the individuality of some of his characters, described by him as living at the edge of their existence, the relationship becomes in a sense more profoundly social than psychological in its significance, more concerned at times with territory than with sex. Freud's belief that sexual behavior takes primary motivation with the individual but does not possess the unifying factor of the "demands of self preservation"[13] is clarifying here.

> In one way the neuroses show a striking and far reaching correspondence with the great social productions of art, religion and philosophy, while again they seem like distortions of them. We may say that hysteria is a caricature of an artistic creation, a compulsion neurosis a caricature of a religion, and a paranoiac delusion a caricature of a philosophic system. In the last analysis this deviation goes back to the fact that the neuroses are asocial formations; they seek to accomplish by private means what arose in society through collective labour. In analysing the impulse of the neuroses one learns that motive powers of sexual origin exercise the determining influence in them, while the corresponding cultural creations rest upon social impulses and on such as have issued from the combination of egotistical and sexual components.[14]

The ritual patterning of Pinter's drama, then, partly turns what may look like very neurotic behavior into behavior with a wider social significance and application. It also may account for the occasional predominance of the territorial imperative over the sexual as its focus; *The Caretaker* and *The Dwarfs*, for example, are plays in which women do not figure directly as characters.

The peculiar power of Pinter's treatment of women, however, lies in the ritual counterpoint in the plays rather than in their realistic or ritualistic elements alone. Rose's dilemma in *The Room* is perfectly real and concrete, but we do not learn of her past as we learn of the past of a Blanche DuBois, with her tragic relationship with a homosexual husband, her dying relatives, and her dying land. Emphasis moves away from psychological explanation to ritual exploration as Rose's tea and breakfast ceremonies act in counterpart to her sacrifice in the eternal battle between father and son or father and husband for the woman.

But if Pinter's dramas succeed most when their ritual counterpoint is at its fullest, his least successful portrayal of the sexual relationship is in his most conventional drama, *A Night Out*. In this three-act play, originally produced on radio (March 1, 1960) and then on television (April 24, 1960), psychological explanation replaces his more usual use of ritual exploration. The play is an overstatement of Pinter's recurrent identification of woman as mother and whore.

A Night Out revolves around the relationship between Albert Stokes and his mother. Albert, the stereotype rather than the archetype of the mama's boy, comes to a crucial juncture in his life when he attends an office party on a night he would ordinarily spend at home with his mother playing rummy. Unable to spare her son for a single "night out," Mrs. Stokes concentrates on trying to get him to "put the bulb in Grandma's room"[15] though, as Albert reminds her, Grandma has been dead for ten years. Such nice detail does not save the play from a caricature of a possessive mother, as such over-clear exchanges as the following reveal:

> MOTHER: Your father would turn in his grave if he heard you raise your voice to me. You're all I've got, Albert. I want you to remember that. I haven't got anyone else. I want you . . . I want you to bear that in mind.
> ALBERT: I'm sorry . . . I raised my voice. (P. 6)

When Albert is accused at the party of taking liberties with a lady (the offender is really the elderly, senile Ryan, in whose honor the party is given), he gets into a fight with an accuser who actually calls him a "mother's boy." Unable to really rebel against his mother, Albert returns home; and the audience is allowed to wonder if he actually hits her with the clock he lifts for the purpose.

In the following scene, Albert is picked up by a girl who poses as a dignified mother and picks at him much as his own mother does. But Albert sees through her pretense; the picture of her little girl is really herself, and she is no mother at all, only a prostitute. Yet Albert's ineffectual bullying of the girl only echoes his ineffectual treatment of his mother, who is alive and sadistically forgiving at the play's end.

What Albert has come to see, however, is a true likeness between his mother and the whore. "You're all the same, you see, you're all the same, you're just a dead weight round my neck," he blurts out at the girl, identifying her nagging with his mother's. "You haven't got any breeding. She hadn't either. And what about those girls tonight? Same kind. And that one. I didn't touch her!" (p. 43).

Albert is as unable to touch a girl as he is to resist his mother. Horrified but held by his own mother's seductive possessiveness, he is caught in the toils of a love-hate relationship that is almost a documented case history—rare for Pinter's drama—of an Oedipus complex.

Pinter's recurrent identification of mother and whore appears also in *The Birthday Party*, in which Stanley's relationship with Meg is very similar to Albert's relationship with his mother. Stanley, though he flinches beneath Meg's blatantly sensuous possessiveness, is unable to break away. In that play, however, the relationship becomes part of the ritual sacrifice of Stanley as scapegoat, and Meg's behavior is part of her role as a tragi-comic fertility goddess. Albert and Mrs. Stokes of *A Night Out* are too conventional to move in such mythical dimension; they remain one-dimensional. Mrs. Stokes is seen as totally destructive, almost, indeed, as caricatured as an Albee "Mommy."

The Basement tends to go to the other extreme. If the Albert-mother relationship in *A Night Out* remains naturalistic and stereotyped in conception, *The Basement* is almost pure ritual, with little attempt at realistic character development. The men who battle for apartment and girl seem in this play "subject to the revolving of some eternal triangle, . . . more like automata than people."[16]

Here too the woman in the play is seen as a whore, switching with abandon from Stott to Law, even turning to smile at Law from the bed she shares with Stott. Law considers her a whore and betrays to his rival her seductive actions to him, but curiously, it is the defeated Law who gets the girl in this drama.

In Frazer's theory, the successors to the priesthood of Nemi were all allied with the goddess of the grove whom they served.[17] The girl's alliance with the victim rather than the victor in *The Basement* is a variation on the Golden Bough ritual, for mother earth is scorned, banished with the victim, even as Clytemnestra was killed with her usurping Aegisthus. There are indications, however, that the victim is also victor in the play, or at least that he has been a usurper. Stott, moving in on Law, seems to be the usurper, but the play gives evidence of a continuous cycle in which Stott and Law alternately possess the basement apartment, the evicted man taking the girl.

Because the ritual is so nakedly and visually emphasized in *The Basement*, the play, though an arresting piece, lacks the complexity of the masterly one-act drama *A Slight Ache*. In the earlier drama Flora's role as fertility goddess is developed with elegant ritual counterpoint—the English matron juxtaposed with the archetypal goddess of earth—as Pinter makes his comment on modern British life and the primitive ongoing rhythms of life as well (see chapter 3).

In *Tea Party* (1965), a television drama based on an earlier short story and reminiscent of *A Slight Ache*, women are seen once more at the center of the ritual transfer of power. When asked what the play was about, Pinter said it was the "story of a business man's reaction to his new secretary and the effect she has on him."[18] Disson is head of a prosperous business selling sanitary ware—"more bidets than anyone else in England."[19] He hires a new secretary the day before his second marriage, and his relationship with her runs parallel to his relationship with his wife and family. Behind the amusing pack of clichés that he calls his life lurks a self-doubting, lustful man who "touches" his provocative and sensual secretary as she playfully protests her previous employer has done. The play reveals Disson becoming obsessed with his hidden, dying self, which his secretary is bringing to the fore.

The clichés with which Disson has built his life involve efficiency, communication, and interdependence, with efficiency firmly cutting him off from the communication and interdependence that he calls indispensable. "I think I should explain to you the sort of man I am," he tells his newly hired brother-in-law, Willy.

> I'm a thorough man. I like things to be done and done well. I don't like dithering. I don't like indulgence. I don't like self-doubt. I don't like fuzziness. I like clarity. Clear intention. Precise execution. . . . That's why your sister loves me. I don't play about at the periphery of matters. I go right to the center. (Pp. 52-53)

Disson's development of a visual problem has less tragic overtones than Edward's "slight ache" in his eyes because Disson has become almost a living parody of the efficient business world; his domineering, hollow phrases preclude any real contact or understanding with Willy, his wife, or his children by a previous marriage. The children, John and Tom, inhabit their father's cliché-ridden world and comment only briefly on its hollowness when their new stepmother, Diana, tells them how much they mean to their father.

JOHN: Children seem to mean a great deal to their parents, I've noticed. Though I've often wondered what "a great deal" means.

TOM: I've often wondered what "mean" means. (P. 55)

Ronald Hayman finds Disson, the blind and bandaged victim at his own tea party, less convincing than the blindfolded Stanley at his birthday party because Disson would never "choose himself as a victim or see himself as a failure,"[20] whereas Stanley does. At least, Hayman concludes, the play does not concern itself with "exploring or explaining"[21] such a self-conception. Fortunately, the play does not explain Disson as victim, but it certainly does explore him as such. Aside from the hollowness of his clichés and his overprotestation of strength, Disson encourages the very forces that threaten him, promoting the brother-in-law who has toasted him at the wedding by praising Diana, who has taken Diana as his secretary with all the overtones of "touching" that such an arrangement suggests in the play, and who would take Disson's own secretary, Wendy, as well. The short story on which the play is based was told from Disson's point of view, and the play too is written very much from his angle: the audience feels the impact of the forces bearing down on Disson as if they were sharing his nightmare.

In *Tea Party*, women are divided, at first as wife—the dignified Diana who loves Disson for his strength and certitude—and whore—the seductive secretary who plays the role of earth mother to Disson and likes him for his weakness and childishness. "I always feel like kissing you when you've got that on round your eyes," Wendy assures Disson, who has her chiffon round his eyes. "Do you know that? Because you're all in the dark" (p. 79). As the play progresses, however, and Willy seems to have won all for himself, reigning as new king at the anniversary tea party, both Diana and Wendy, now allied, are envisioned as Willy's to do with what he will, as whores.

Hinchcliffe finds the epigraph for the original short-story version of *Tea Party* ("In the country of the blind he found himself a king")[22] inappropriate, but in ritual terms the epigraph is exact and illuminating for the play as well. Here again are all the signs of the dying king-god, the seasonal year demon. The play covers exactly one year, beginning with Disson's marriage and ending with his first anniversary and his fall. The wife, who appears at first in all her dignity, gradually assumes the aspect of whore, merging her role with that of the sensual secretary because inevitably the wife is allied with the new king. Diana, the goddess of the grove of Nemi, also might have assumed the aspect of whore to the reigning king, who knew of her inevitable treachery to him. That the new alliance in *Tea Party* has incestuous overtones is understandable too. "Tell me about the place where you two were born. Where you played at being brother and sister" (p. 73), the suspicious Disson asks Willy. Here are overtones of the Oedipal conflict that informs the seasonal rituals, though in *Tea Party*, the opposing son is seen as a brother.

But why is Disson a king in the "country of the blind"? Echoes of H. G. Wells's story "The Country of the Blind" provide ironical associations, for Disson's aspirations are crushed even as the sighted hero of the Wells tale finds himself helpless amidst the blind. But it is Disson who loses his sight in *Tea Party*, not the others. In the short-story version, however, all the characters wore spectacles, suggesting a generally myopic society over which Disson has reigned. Enough of the tragic rhythm, discussed in relationship to *A Slight Ache* in chapter 3, remains in the play to suggest that Disson's failing sight masks his growing insight into the true nature of his surroundings and himself. Like Sophocles' Oedipus, Disson is most kingly when he is dispossessed, most aware when he is totally blind.

Disson's awareness, unlike Oedipus' or even Edward's in *A Slight Ache*, is almost inarticulate in the play, placing him nearer to the early victim, Stanley. Stanley, however, tried to evade the society that would make him conform, whereas Disson has consented to reign over that society as arch-conformist and is hence seen as much a victim of himself as of others. His spiritual death becomes even more ludicrous than Stanley's; the orgy that accompanies it is set not at a birthday party but at a tea party in his super-sanitary office with its atmosphere of lifeless sterility. The satirical thrust of the play is evident as the modern business magnate and the society over which he rules are almost caricatured. The play, then, seems to lie somewhere be-tween *A Slight Ache* and *The Birthday Party*; its ritual counterpoint suggests the cyclical persistence of a society that is at once parodied and infused with new life, a society of the blind with its king who finally cannot bear to see and its queen who is inevitably wife and whore.

Woman is again portrayed as wife and whore in two other television plays by Pinter, *The Collection* (1961) and *The Lover* (1963). These plays share with the drama of Pirandello a sense of the elusiveness of reality. The series of views on the nature of an alleged affair between Stella and Bill in *The Collection* is never resolved into a "right" view, and one is left with something of the effect of Piran-dello's *Right You Are If You Think You Are*. The tightrope Richard and Sarah walk in *The Lover* as they straddle the world of fantasy and reality—husband and wife by night and lovers by day—is not unlike the tightrope walked by Pirandello's Henry IV, who cannot escape from the reality of his fantasy. Pinter shares with Pirandello, and with much of modern drama since that prophetic writer, a sense of the elusiveness and fragmentary nature of identity.

In *The Collection*, Stella's husband of two years attempts a confrontation with Bill, with whom Stella has confessed a passing affair indulged in at a recent dress showing at Leeds. Bill first denies the affair, then gives a different ver-sion of it with Stella as seducer, and finally suggests they merely talked about what they would do. Stella, at the play's end, strokes her kitten and will not tell.

The truth, however, lies not in the reality or fantasy of the affair so much as it lies in the relationships that are revealed in James's quest for the truth. Stella's alleged lover Bill is engaged in a homosexual relationship with Harry, an elegant gentleman who has picked him up in a slum. Harry is intensely jealous of James, with whom Bill plays in a seductive and hostile fashion. James, apparently tempted by Bill, vengefully thanks his wife for opening up a new world to him as if she has given him nothing else in their relationship, and the three men play out their mutual jealousies in games, mock duels with fruit knives that draw blood but leave them curiously unsatisfied. The point is that all the characters are deeply shaken about themselves, that they clearly cannot know themselves or Stella absolutely.[23]

Walter Kerr, who admires Pinter for his Pirandellian conception of character as potential rather than as something fixed, suggests that the playwright's recurrent use of the "whore" image in his plays is his way of seeing the fluidity of identity. The whore "by definition, lacks definition,"[24] he suggests. "Existentially speaking; we are all life's whores to the degree that we are in motion and have not arbitrarily codified and thereby stilled ourselves."[25]

Pinter may indeed concentrate on the whore because she is "unknown," but he goes beyond this Pirandellian sense of man's eternally becoming, fragmented identity as the whore plays her ritual role—a role that, within limits, is defined. The two disturbed relationships in *The Collection* reveal the three men in their incomplete sexuality stalking one another in a super-sophisticated jungle with Stella, the fertility goddess, who for the first time is seen to be suffering in her role. Must she become a whore and serve the incumbent to the throne—the slum child rising in the world through Harry's attentions? Is she to be the un-

known enigma to the Golden Bough priests who battle
with one another for ascendancy and possibly for her, but
more for themselves? Pinter said that, after seeing the play
for some time, his sympathies were with Stella, alone with
her cat.[26] Flora, the self-satisfied, humorous fertility goddess of A Slight Ache, is replaced in this play by a suffering
goddess whose riddle and enigma is the tragedy she endures in the midst of the male comedy that surrounds her.

Once more, Pinter employs the primitive ritual role of
fertility goddess, wife and whore, in ritual counterpoint—
a brilliant comment on modern life in its understated so-
phistication and on ancient archetypal relationships of
man and woman at the same time.

> What is astute in Pinter's handling of his subject is that
> nearly all the impulses involved are only partially expressed
> and thus emerge only as possibilities. There can be no Othello
> or Iago in such a situation because modern men (and wom-
> en) disapprove of jealousy and the acts of violence arising
> from it. They therefore attempt to repress them so that
> finally they (and we) begin to doubt the reality of their feel-
> ings. Am I really "fit to be tied" because my wife has been
> unfaithful? Can my contact with that man be really consid-
> ered "an affair," or did I just toy with the idea of such a con-
> tact? If I were certain that he or she had an affair would I
> divorce, maim or murder, or would I go on living with my
> mate in tortured or "sophisticated" indecision, the possible
> infidelity forgotten or forgiven because I am unsure whether
> I also transgressed?[27]

Amid talk of olives and church bells, then, Bill almost dares
but doesn't. And Stella remains enigmatic, smiling, an isolated modern woman with her cat, an ancient riddling
sphinx playing her tragi-comic role.

If the woman in The Collection is treated with sympathy
in her double role as whore-wife, the role of the woman as
wife-whore becomes the very subject of The Lover. This
television play explores the tensions that arise when Richard challenges his relationship with his wife Sarah, who

for years has been his wife by night and his lover by day. As in *The Collection*, the fragmented nature of life is explored as Richard comes to view his wife-mistress as a whore and he himself plays various roles within roles, his role as lover divided between that of attacker and protector. But as the play concentrates on Richard's desire to integrate the roles played by himself and his wife, Sarah's need to continue their compartmentalized existence is fully examined. Her need, in fact, proves stronger and dominates as the play ends.

We are given no psychological explanations for the couple's role-playing and sexual games in the play; their odd behavior is in no respect treated as a study in neurosis. Rather, Pinter makes his modern British suburban couple enact their ritual of love in counterpoint with the ritual of their married life together, the alternation of roles suggesting at once the fragmented nature of modern life and the archetypal, eternally divided role of the female.

The play gains its humor from an understated acceptance of Sarah's lover by her briefcase-wielding, cheek-kissing husband departing for work. We do not yet know that husband and lover are one.

RICHARD: (*Amiably.*) Is your lover coming today?
SARAH: Mmnn.
RICHARD: What time?
SARAH: Three.
RICHARD: Will you be going out . . . or staying in?
SARAH: Oh . . . I think we'll stay in.
RICHARD: I thought you wanted to go to that exhibition.
SARAH: I did, yes . . . but I think I'd prefer to stay in with him today.
RICHARD: Mmnn-hmmm. Well, I must be off.
(*He goes to hall and puts on his bowler hat.*)
Will he be staying long, do you think?
SARAH: Mmmnnn . . .
RICHARD: About . . . six, then.

SARAH: Yes.
RICHARD: Have a pleasant afternoon.
SARAH: Mmnn.
RICHARD: Bye-bye.[28]

If the lover did not turn out to be the husband, the understated acceptance of him by Richard might lead into a parody on the passionless, understated life of the English living a life of convenience and ritual comfort. The introduction of Richard as lover and then as husband jealous of himself as lover, however, suggests passionate undercurrents. As the couple enact their passion with the primitive beating of fingers on bongo drums and an appropriate change of clothing and roles, their passion reveals a more instinctive and primitive side to their lives, which threatens to break out of the compartment of life in which they have kept it. The ritual counterpoint of lovemaking with homemaking suggests the problematical nature of modern homemaking, which can become a comfortable and sterile decoration. Richard speaks of his pride in his wife and her "command of contemporary phraseology" and her "delicate use of the very latest idiomatic expression, so subtly employed" (p. 31) as if she were a handy possession. But the counterpoint suggests as well the age-old role of woman as fertility goddess, wife to the old god and the new—and hence, whore.

Perhaps Sarah's desire to keep her roles of wife and mistress separate (she does not accept the role of whore) is her way of trying to defeat time, the eternal cycle of life enacted in other Pinter dramas. By playing both roles with her own husband, Sarah removes the need for a new god or king. Richard is both, and hence she will remain forever faithful to her husband, even as she will remain forever alluring to her lover, if only they may remain the same person. And they may only remain the same, she apparently feels, if the roles are kept separate. Hence, Pinter comments wryly in his play on the relationship of the sexes, on modern attitudes toward women, and on the ambiguous nature of her role at all times.

The ambiguous nature of women is the subject as well of Pinter's 1963 film version of Penelope Mortimer's novel *The Pumpkin Eater*. Once again Pinter deals with a fertility goddess, but here she is more the earth mother, mother-wife, than wife-whore.

The conflict between husband and children is overwhelming to Jo (played by Anne Bancroft), who is working on her third marriage and eighth child. Pinter removes much of the psychological explanation of the novel as well as its introspection, moving, as it were, outside the novel and looking in.[29] When Philip Oakes commends the film's director Jack Clayton for avoiding a casebook style and for capturing "something of all marriages"[30] in the scrutiny of this particular one, he doubtless has Pinter's script partly to thank.

Pinter's exploration of the eternal mother, with its curious echoes of Virginia Woolf's *Mrs. Dalloway* and *To the Lighthouse*, is set in a modern sophisticated world with which his character can hardly cope. Her nervous breakdown takes place at Harrod's, for example, and she is threatened by a hysterical woman while imprisoned under the drier at a beauty parlor. Once again the veneer of the secular rituals of parties, shopping tours, and so on, works in counterpoint with primitive undercurrents, which erupt finally into a savage physical fight between husband and wife. "Some of the behavior of Peter Finch and Anne Bancroft is so primitively savage—and I don't mean only the clawing, slapping, tearing, pinching fight they have together—that we feel they might be wearing animal skins."[31] Jo, however, takes her place with Pinter's other sympathetic portrayals of women divided between the multiple roles which sometimes do reduce them to primitive behavior.

Perhaps the most complex and moving of Pinter's tragi-comic heroines, though, is Ruth, who combines the roles of wife, mother, and whore in Pinter's three-act drama, *The Homecoming* (1965). Here Pinter's focus is clearly on the fertility goddess and her place in the ritual renewal of life.

On a realistic plane, Ruth's behavior in the play is both shocking and bizarre. Spurning her professor husband and her respected and comfortable life with him and their three children in America, Ruth turns to her husband's family with whom they are visiting in England and decides to stay with them. She dances with her husband's brother Lenny and kisses him, rolls on the couch with his brother Joey, and contracts to stay on with her father-in-law Max and family as general housekeeper, prostitute, and mother —all before her husband's eyes and finally with his consent. Realistically speaking, such macabre behavior is only comprehensible if Ruth is regarded as a nymphomaniac whom her husband willingly unloads.

Pinter, however, has not conceived Ruth as a neurotic, realistic character, although she is deeply troubled. Even on a realistic plane, her actions make a certain amount of sense, and on a poetic and ritual plane, they become clear and fascinating in their significance.

Teddy, Ruth's husband, is the intellectual in the play who is contrasted with the crude family with whom he has broken. Max, his father, is an ex-butcher, whose shaky rule of the family is challenged by Ruth. Lenny, his elder brother, is a pimp, and Joey, his younger brother, is a demolition worker in training to be a boxer. The family picture is completed by Max's brother Sam, a chauffeur, whose generally passive role in the drama is not unlike Teddy's. The dead mother Jessie is constantly evoked by the entire family, who live in an atmosphere of open hostility that is extended to Ruth. Max greets Ruth as a slut who will replace his wife.

Max: I haven't seen the bitch for six years, he comes home
without a word, he brings a filthy scrubber off the street,
he shacks up in my house!

Teddy: She's my wife! We're married!

Pause.

Max: I've never had a whore under this roof before. Ever
since your mother died. . . . They come back from America, they bring the slopbucket with them. They bring the
bedpan with them. (*To Teddy.*) Take that disease away
from me. Get her away from me.[32]

Ruth, however, is less perturbed with Max's welcome
than with her husband's attitude toward her and life.
Perhaps she understands her father-in-law's crude bluster
as the true welcome it soon becomes. Jessie, whom he
hated, loved, and needed, is alternately idealized as an
angel and berated as a bitch and whore by Max; and Ruth
is more than willing to play the double role in which he
correctly casts her. Teddy, on the other hand, is a dead
man; and Ruth has experienced a near death in her relationship with him. Teddy operates, he explains, "on things
and not in things" (p. 61). His critical works, beyond the
comprehension of his family, are based on this power of
his to remain uninvolved. "You're just objects," he tells his
family. "You just . . . move about. I can observe it. I can
see what you do. It's the same as I do. But you're lost in it.
You won't get me being . . . I won't be lost in it" (p. 62).

Life with Teddy, then, has held no reality for Ruth, who
rejects Teddy's noninvolvement for the movement of life.
When Lenny tries to engage Teddy in philosophical discussion about the nature of being, Teddy hedges about
what is in his province; but Ruth enters the discussion even
as she chooses to enter the family.

Don't be too sure though. You've forgotten something. Look
at me, I . . . move my leg. That's all it is. But I wear . . .
underwear . . . which moves with me . . . it . . . captures your attention. Perhaps you misinterpret. The action is

simple. It's a leg . . . moving. My lips move. Why don't you
restrict . . . your observation to that? Perhaps the fact that
they move is more significant . . . than the words which
come through them. You must bear that . . . possibility
. . . in mind. (Pp. 52-53)

Ruth follows this declaration for sheer instinctual being
with a description of America as a wasteland, a desert.
"It's all rock," she says. "And sand. It stretches . . . so far
. . . everywhere you look. And there's lots of insects there"
(p. 53). Ruth has come home to England thirsty as from a
desert, and her embracing of the family shows the measure
of her thirst for life that persists in her and has died in her
husband. In a crucial scene with Lenny, who has given
Ruth a glass of water that he then wishes to take away,
Ruth refuses the glass and says, "If you take the glass . . .
I'll take you" (p. 34). Flustered by what he considers
"some kind of proposal" (p. 34), Lenny loses the round as
Ruth drains the glass. "Oh, I was thirsty" (p. 35), she explains, and the rest of the play continues to reveal the
depths of that thirst as she proceeds to take Lenny and his
family on. Perhaps the action of the play may be described
as Ruth's escape from the desert (America and Teddy) to
the jungle (London and Teddy's family). At any rate, it is
clearly Ruth who comes home and Teddy who must leave.

In many ways, then, *The Homecoming* moves in a parallel vein with *A Slight Ache*. Like Edward in the one-act
play, Teddy is the cliché-ridden philosopher who has become old and impotent before his time. "Winter'll soon be
upon us. Time to renew one's wardrobe," Lenny remarks;
and Ruth agrees that "that's a good thing to do" (p. 56).
The fertility goddess must look to the new god and new
year, forsaking the old as the seasons change; and Teddy
is brushed off by the family as a fallen leaf.

If the new god appears in the guise of Max and family, an
impotent crew basically hostile to women, he is no less dis-
turbing than the old broken-down matchseller who comes

to replace Edward. Once again, Pinter's view of the ritual renewal is a dark one; the choices are not between good and evil but between life and death. Ruth will be a mother to Joey, who is satisfied to "not go the whole hog" (p. 68) if he can have her love. (Roger Pierce suggests Joey is more virginal than impotent in the play,[33] which, if true, makes him the best candidate for the new god.) She will be a whore for Lenny and take care of the house and the sexual needs of the family as well. She will be a wife to Max, displacing him, however, as she takes over as matriarch of the family. The deal completed, Sam, who recognizes the reincarnation of Jessie in Ruth's combined role as whore-wife-mother, blurts out his long-harbored secret that "Mac-Gregor had Jessie in the back of my cab as I drove them along" (p. 78), and collapses. He is unable to accept the image of woman so corrupted or of himself even passively involved in that corruption. Once again, the play is hardly an unqualified celebration.

Ruth's choice is indeed a complex one, and Pinter views it in the ritual counterpoint of the play with a combination of bitter satire and celebration. Ruth is better equipped to deal with the jungle than the desert and operates with her new family not only with all the barbarity of primitive passion but with the barbarity of civilization as well. Civilization is seen at its most cynical when Ruth closes the deal on her new relationships with the "contract ritual" of modern life, which moves in bitterly hilarious counterpoint with the primitive ritual movement that the contract designates.

> Ruth: I'd need an awful lot. Otherwise I wouldn't be content.
> Lenny: You'd have everything.
> Ruth: I would naturally want to draw up an inventory of everything I would need, which would require your signatures in the presence of witnesses.
> Lenny: Naturally.

RUTH: All aspects of the agreement and conditions of employment would have to be clarified to our mutual satisfaction before we finalized the contract.

LENNY: Of course. (Pp. 77-78)

The nature of the homecomer is further illustrated when we see Ruth at the end of the play: the enigmatic sphinx who Max fears has not gotten it clear. "She'll use us, she'll make use of us, I can tell you! I can smell it! You want to bet?" (p. 81), Max says, the play ending with his plea on bended knee for a kiss. Like Flora, Ruth has not only discarded one husband for a new one but reigns at the play's end as fertility goddess, in full control of the situation. The priest of Nemi, one recalls, is but a guard in the sacred grove of Diana.

The Homecoming differs from *A Slight Ache,* however, in its ritual implications, as the focus moves from the discarded husband to the wife. Our sympathies are enlisted for the dying Edward in *A Slight Ache;* but Teddy is already dead when *The Homecoming* begins, and our attention and sympathies are focused instead on Ruth. Ruth, like Flora, would avoid the whole situation if possible, suggesting to Teddy that they leave even before they are greeted, just as Flora would ignore the intrusive matchseller. Doubtless the two women sense the nature of the ritual to be undergone and the agonizing sacrifice at its center. But if the men initiate the ritual in each situation, Ruth no less than Flora ends by embracing the role that she must play; and the drama focuses continually on her often unstated feelings as she officiates at and endures the play's ritual renewal.

If Edward was both victim and victor in *A Slight Ache,* this double role of victim and victor is assumed by Ruth rather than Teddy in *The Homecoming.* True, Teddy has victimized Ruth by offering her only a sterile, unreal life in America (Michael Craig, who created the role, said, "He's an awful man, Teddy. He's rationalized his aggressions, but underneath he's Eichmann."),[34] and he is discarded in turn by Ruth. The play, however, focuses less on Teddy as scapegoat, who seems content with taking Lenny's cheese roll in exchange for his wife, than on Ruth, who in a much fuller capacity enacts the victim-victor role.

As victim Ruth has clearly suffered as the partner of a dead man who praises her in the empty conventionalized phrases that are a measure of his ignorance of her individuality.

> She's a great help to me over there. She's a wonderful wife and mother. She's a very popular woman. She's got lots of friends. It's a great life, at the University . . . you know . . . it's a very good life. We've got a lovely house . . . we've got all . . . we've got everything we want. It's a very stimulating environment. (P. 50)

Ruth, though, has not had what she wants in what to her is a deadening environment. Her prior life as a model "for the body," suggestive of prostitution, involved modeling at times outdoors near a lake; and despite the element of victimization in such a life, the lake on which she dwells wistfully, like the glass of water she drains in the contest with Lenny, has obviously sustained her in the past. Her acceptance of her role as a whore-mother-wife in the new family, then, is both degrading and sustaining to Ruth. She will suffer the insults of her new family—"she's a tart" (p. 58), Joey tells his father in front of her—accepting the role of the beloved and detested Jessie because it fulfills her hunger and thirst for sex and her desire to be needed. And the men need her in a far deeper sense than Teddy does, for they are still alive and struggling.

As Ruth becomes the central sacrificial victim of the play, she becomes the central figure of divinity as well. Rising from the couch on which she has submitted as victim to Joey's advances, Ruth becomes the imperious victor, demanding food and drink and finally making her contract

with the family very much on her own terms. Ruth has replaced Jessie, just as the matchseller replaced Edward, and
Lenny and Joey have replaced Teddy and Max. Rose, the
victim of *The Room*, was called home and could not come.
Ruth comes home as victim and stays as victim-victor.

The play's richness derives partly from the double ritual
movement in which Teddy and Ruth are both sacrificed
and Ruth and possibly Lenny and Joey are reborn. Lenny
is the play's true philosopher, always questioning everyone
in the self-mocking manner of Mick in *The Caretaker* and
covering his own sensitivity by his crude banter, but nevertheless revealing his suffering spirit of inquiry. Lenny
greets his returning brother with his sleeplessness: "It's
just that something keeps waking me up. Some kind of
tick" (p. 25). In his first interchange with Ruth, Lenny
refuses to agree with his brother's identification of the tick-
ing sound as the clock.

> The trouble is I'm not all that convinced it was the clock. I
> mean there are lots of things which tick in the night, don't
> you find that? All sorts of objects, which, in the day, you
> wouldn't call anything else but commonplace. They give you
> no trouble. But in the night any given one of a number of
> them is liable to start letting out a bit of a tick. . . . (P. 28)

Lenny might be describing the play's action with his
awareness of life's undercurrents, the impending doom
which lurks beneath the commonplace, that old weasel of
Pinter's under the cocktail cabinet.

Lenny's philosophical questioning of the reluctant
Teddy on the essence of life also has sincere undercurrents,
and his crude questioning of his father about the night of
his conception is particularly revealing.

> I'll tell you what, Dad, since you're in the mood for a bit of a
> . . . chat, I'll ask you a question. It's a question I've been
> meaning to ask you for some time. That night . . . you know
> . . . the night you got me . . . that night with Mum, what

was it like? Eh? When I was just a glint in your eye. What was it like? What was the background to it? I mean, I want to know the real facts about my background. I mean, for instance, is it a fact that you had me in mind all the time, or is it a fact that I was the last thing you had in mind? (P. 36)

In *Myth and Reality*, Eliade discusses the need for man to dwell on his beginnings, which provide him with a model or source of renewal. If, as he suggests, "the return to origins gives the hope of rebirth,"[35] Lenny's curiosity about his own begetting as well as his general curiosity about life reveals his search for renewal in the wasteland he inhabits. Beneath the mask of the sadistic pimp is the frightened child seeking in the darkness of his life for what might hopefully be more ideal origins in some long-lost paradise. He seeks vainly too for a mother's love in the woman whom he recognizes with ambivalence as his slut-mother of old.

"*The Homecoming*," writes Richard Schechner, "is a probe of the dark male attitudes toward the 'mother-whore' and the equally compelling female desire to play this double role."[36] Once again Pinter probes into such universal attitudes and desires with that ritual counterpoint which juxtaposes modern life with that which is ancient and universal. The play's secular rituals—Ruth serving tea, the men smoking cigars—move in counterpoint with the ritual sacrifice and renewal which transpires amidst this "taking of a toast and tea."

Pinter, it would seem, cares deeply for all of the lost characters of his drama who he admits act "pretty horribly" but always, he says, "out of the texture of their lives and for other reasons which are not evil but slightly desperate."[37] His sympathetic portrayal of Stella and Sarah and his humorous portrayal of Flora have led him in this play, moreover, to dwell on his own version of that alien biblical Ruth who comes home in despair and makes her desperate choice for life. At their best Pinter's women do more than struggle for power; they struggle for life. And if

within that struggle they act as destroyer as well as preserver, as wife, mother, and whore, perhaps, after all, they
fulfill Pinter's honest and unflinching vision of what life is.

Although the focus shifts back to the male in Pinter's
1967 film adaptation of Nicolas Mosley's novel, *The Accident*, Anna (played by Jacqueline Sassard) is strongly
reminiscent of Ruth in *The Homecoming*. Like Ruth, the
suffering Anna, a lovely and exotic Australian student at
Oxford, supplies the needs of the various men in her life.
She is potential mistress, whore, and earth mother to her
tutor Stephen, sensitively interpreted by Dirk Bogard, who
had worked with the Pinter-Losey combination in *The
Servant*. She is potential wife to Stephen's aristocratic student, William, and becomes engaged to him. And she is
mistress to Charlie, one of Stephen's more extroverted col-
leagues.

Stephen takes Anna after the accident which kills her
fiancé—an accident which begins and ends the film, and is
in a sense no accident at all but an inevitable part of the
ritual that patterns the film. His wife Rosalind (played by
Pinter's wife, Vivien Merchant), struggles alone to give
birth to their third child even as Stephen strives to recap-
ture his vanishing youth by living out his desires with
Anna. It is as if Stephen must explore woman in all of her
potential roles, as wife, mother, and whore, before he can
give up Anna and return to his home, his wife, and himself.

If *The Accident* involves the battle of possession for a
woman and for youth and for self, the film medium allows
that battle to work itself out in subtle character development and a patterning of time sequence that more fully
suppresses the nightmare that erupts into Pinter's dramas
and maintains a strong naturalistic surface until the end.
Beneath that surface the battle exacts its victims—all suffer
in the film, and William dies; but in no other Pinter play
or film is the resolution as richly suggestive of a renewal
of life almost unqualified by the bitterness of battle. The

film suggests a fuller celebration of life, a greater acceptance of it, than any other work that Pinter has attempted
thus far.

Stephen is a philosopher of another order than the dried-
up Teddy of *The Homecoming* or the tortured and impotent Lenny. *The Accident's* hero, rather, is an intelligent,
inquiring, emotional man married to a sensitive and understanding wife; and out of the awareness of the couple
new life emerges triumphantly. The ritual is there, bizarre
in the details of the accident and the subsequent "taking"
of Anna, savage as the game (a kind of football) played
by the male guests at William's aristocratic, ancestral home,
and clear in the battle literally to the death between Stephen and William for possession; but Stephen is able to
make something of the ritual—to find new meaning for his
life and to truly rejoice in it.

Pinter's hero in the film is a touch more alienated than
Mosley's hero in the novel, less able to talk with his wife,
less sure of the life of their new child at the end. Some of
the reasons for keeping Anna at his house and protecting
her from the police are obscured in the film, which accentu-
ates the final ritual movement over the naturalistic surface.
Still, Pinter has worked with a book which has given him
the more hopeful characters with whom he works and a
very conscious ritual base (the book, as no Pinter play,
refers specifically to its action in terms of fertility rites and
earth mothers); hence, it is difficult to determine how
much of the celebration is his, how much Mosley's.

Pinter, however, has remained essentially faithful to his
own themes and techniques in *The Accident*, as he has in
his other films. And he may even have found through Mosley's Stephen the key to an opening up of character on a
more complex and tragic level than he had thus far
achieved. It remains difficult, though, to evaluate the film
as Pinter's own because of its faithfulness to the novel.
Perhaps, too, one misses in the film's slightly romantic

treatment of its theme some of the power of the celebration in *The Homecoming*, which is so tautly held in check by the caustic satire of secular rituals that accompany its sacred ritual to its bitter and enigmatic end. And despite the haunting character of the Sphinx-like Anna, she is a character who will vanish from Stephen's life like a dream. Ruth has come home to stay.

Pinter in Production

"If you press me for a definition,
I'd say that what goes on in my plays is realistic,
but what I'm doing is not realism."[1]

Harold Pinter began rehearsals for *The Man in the Glass Booth*, written by his friend Robert Shaw, with the following statement: "This is a play about a Jew who pretends to be a Nazi but is really a Jew."[2] According to Lawrence Pressman, one of the play's actors, the statement received a big laugh from the company because the play is obviously about a great deal more, "but that's Harold." An elaboration of "that's Harold" simply meant that Pinter and the cast "went to work like artists" after this brief introduction, and going to work like artists had little to do with analysis of meanings or symbols in the play. Particular attention was placed rather on specific actions, keeping the action clean, precise, and subtle, with concentration on what is done, not why it's done.

Pinter's directorial approach, with its emphasis on action and interaction, is a nontheorizing one in which the actors are urged to concentrate on the play as reality. Pinter had found the young American actor Pressman amusingly over-intellectual in his approach to *Glass Booth*, and the actor felt that he had learned from Pinter as well as the others in the cast something important about being less theoretical in an effort at self-protection. Theorizing, Pressman suggested, only leads to "showing" things rather than "playing the moment." He himself is a box collector, he explained, and to know why he collects them is irrelevant to the reality of collecting them. A fine actor himself, Pinter understands this and knows how to work with an actor.

Pinter is quite explicit about the reality of the lives of his characters; but the undercurrents beneath the dialogue are not verifiable in his estimation, and the abstracting critic comes under attack for his attempt to pin down the ambiguities. The critic, Pinter complains, puts a character on the shelf as a symbol with the implication that we know what we are up to from birth till death—"an invalid assumption."[3] Perhaps there is something of Socratic humility and pride in this impatience with those who approach the nonverifiable mysterious undercurrents in his plays. The critics think they know what is in the plays, but Pinter is wise because he knows that he does not know. It is important, too, however, to understand Pinter's insistence on his plays as realism as part of the self-protective attitude that Pressman learned from his experience in acting in *The Man in the Glass Booth*. The playwright's reluctance to theorize beyond the present reality, whether it be his work as an actor, director, or writer, doubtless helps him to preserve the basically intuitive approach he takes to his art, to enter deeply into the life of his characters, which he then allows his audience to see.

Such an attitude on Pinter's part should not discourage the attempts of the critic to approach the writer's work any more than Socrates' approach should discourage the inquiring philosopher. It should rather serve as a warning, I believe, to avoid the facile analysis that kills the spirit of a work, or a concentration on symbolic analysis at the expense of the play's reality, which is crucial to the multiple meanings that emerge from a Pinter play. The dramatic critic's task, moreover, it seems to me, should not stop with the script but should follow the writer's work into production. The detection of a ritual counterpoint in Pinter's dramatic world, if it is valid, should have some bearing on the production style of his drama.

Current directors of Pinter's drama tend to agree with his "realistic" approach. Clive Donner, the director of the film version of *The Caretaker*, and Martin Esslin, who is not only an important critic of Pinter's writing but also has been closely involved with radio productions of his work, were in total agreement in separate interviews about the need for a basically realistic or naturalistic approach to Pinter's drama in production. On one level, this insistence on a realistic approach may be accounted for as a directorial technique for any play. Miss Kemp-Welch, who directed the first four television productions of Pinter's work, stated in an interview that she did not think Pinter's plays demanded a special type of production. "They themselves have such a distinctive style," she said, "such a life of their own, that the play itself creates the style—this is true of every great playwright and is not unique to Pinter."[4]

Mr. Esslin was suspicious, too, of my attempt to define a Pinter acting style as an over-academic American approach to the theater,[5] while Donner and Kemp-Welch were dubious about an over-theoretical approach to a production that would attempt to extract symbols instead of portraying a reality. "If a play is symbolic," Miss Kemp-Welch explained, "I do not try to emphasize this by any special means of production. If the production and acting are truthful to the author's intention—the symbolism will be clear and as the author intended."

Alan Schneider, an American director who has worked

with Pinter material, clarifies the current approach to
Pinter production by a general statement about his own
directorial technique. "It is not possible on the stage to be
abstract," he explains. "I'm aware of the philosophical implications of the play [*The Birthday Party*], but I can't
direct philosophical implications." We approach the play,
he added, not realistically, "but with reality."[6] Clive Donner reflects a similar attitude in his refusal to see anything
symbolic in Mick's breaking of his brother's Buddha statue
in *The Caretaker*. To Donner, as a director, this action is
an act of anger and frustration. After all, Mick's brother
would not get moving, Donner said. Continuing to speak
in a "realistic" way about the relationship of the brothers
and the tramp, Donner noted that the brothers cannot talk
to each other. Mick only speaks to Aston once or twice over
the exchange of bags or the dripping from a leak. But at
the end they smile at each other—they are fond of each
other. Aston, he explained, admires Mick's "go" but finds
him a bit pushy, and Mick is fond of Aston but finds him
slow. Aston does not talk much, but he says everything in
a few speeches; and the tramp smells, but he is a human
being. It all works simply. You find the basic emotional
values. The main interest is in people. It is only technically
difficult.[7]

The echoes of Pinter's own approach are clear. Over-
theorizing and symbol hunting can obscure the life of a
play and inhibit the basically intuitive directorial approach
that will find its clues in the text. Pinter says:

> On the whole I would agree that actors and directors
> searching for legitimate psychological motivation in my char-
> acters would get themselves nowhere fast . . . I suppose I
> invariably say, "play the text." . . . What they are is implicit
> in what they say. Certainly it is valid and necessary to ex-
> amine what they do not say and why they do not say what
> they cannot say at the particular time of saying and not say-
> ing.[8]

Pinter's plays do give the director and actor the clues which are needed for playing the silences as well as the spoken words. Donner's description of the relationship between the brothers in *The Caretaker* is a good example of such a reading of the text. The fact that neither Donner nor Kemp-Welch finds Pinter obscure may be due to the completeness of the line of development in the text. When Donner once complimented the actor, Donald Pleasence, on his portrayal in *The Caretaker*, the actor too insisted that it was all in the text, an attitude reflected as well by the director Peter Hall, who likens Pinter to Shakespeare in this respect. "You can't make your own personal comment as an actor," Hall says of Pinter's plays. "You can't cop out. You can't paraphrase Shakespeare and you can't paraphrase Pinter."[9]

Actors and directors working on Pinter plays often find them quite clear, or at least recognizable as life. "I have never found Pinter's plays obscure," Joan Kemp-Welch says. "To me they are devastatingly true and accurate in their observation of life and people." He catches the kind of conversation or lack of it that we all hear and see in a restaurant, for instance, in which the husband and wife may make one remark to one another in a half hour, or one may carry on a nonstop conversation, or neither may talk, both sending silent messages of hate back and forth. Pinter, she said, "uses what human beings do and feel. It is this that he orchestrates in his plays."

I do not believe any of the directors interviewed would suggest Pinter's dramatic world is not complex or mysterious, only that it is not filled with mystifications and not consciously symbolic. Esslin, for example, as adamant as the others on the need to do a Pinter production naturalistically, has certainly been one of the most important critics of Pinter as a poet-realist or absurdist. When he notes that Pinter insists on the reality of his "fantasy" (Ruth does have three children in America in *The Homecoming*), he shows an acute critical awareness of the surrealistic dream elements which inform a Pinter script. When he sides with the other producers of Pinter, however, in insisting on naturalism of set and acting (Losey and Pinter work hand in glove because they are both naturalists, he noted), he too is suggesting the need to play the surface reality that Pinter captures, allowing the other values to arise as they will.

This emphasis on a "realistic" production style does not by any means exclude techniques of production that are oblique or suggestive. Miss Kemp-Welch spoke at length about the need for suggestion in productions, so that those in the audience are able to imagine what they want to see and are not restricted in their imagination by what you show them. This kind of suggestion proved very successful with *The Lover*, she explained, in which many people found the opening hand-play on Bongo drums between the lovers enormously erotic. "In the scene where the lovers crawled under the table to make love, I just showed the top of the table with a bowl of flowers for nearly a minute—many people wrote in to say how dared I show such erotic love making! They had seen nothing but honestly believed they had."

Donner also discusses his own directorial technique as one that makes the audience use their imagination, and Esslin stressed the need for keeping certain ambiguities open in Pinter. One should wonder in *A Slight Ache*, he thought, whether the matchseller really exists or is only a figment of the couple's imagination; and one should wonder in *Night School*, which he had just directed as a radio program in Berlin, whether the young man really does or does not sleep with the girl. The German translation had implied "yes" by a sudden change from the formal use of the personal pronoun (*Sie*) to the intimate form (*Du*). Though Esslin was convinced of the impotency of the character and might share this interpretation with the actor, he felt that it was important to keep the audience wondering.

Hence, even those directors who insist on a realistic approach to a Pinter production exclude neither suggestion nor ambiguity from their techniques of presentation. Neither do they exclude realism as a technique for bringing out other values in the plays. The generally realistic approach to Pinter in production seems based on the idea that careful attention to what realities are given in the text will give the director clues on how to allow the depths of that reality to emerge.

Reviews of Pinter productions, however, have tended to pay more attention to those depths that emerge than to the realistic surface upon which the directors and actors prefer to dwell. Hence, while the producers of Pinter plays often take a realistic approach, the critics often comment on the results as surrealistic, poetic, and ritualistic. Robert Brustein remarks on the "fascinating secular rituals" in Peter Hall's direction of *The Homecoming*, such as the cigar-lighting of the four men that opens the second act and reveals them breaking away "from the central match as if they were opening petals of a carnivourous flower."[10] Warren Sylvester Smith comments too on the effect of *The Homecoming*'s tea scene in which Ruth serves the family tea in "a remarkable ritual, at once solemn and hilarious, a symbol and a sacrament."[11] Clurman also admires Hall's direction of the play because it captures its abstract quality—that quality which goes far beyond the naturalistic. "The pauses or breaks are not elements of character portrayal," Clurman notes, "they are 'freezes' of action to indicate that we are passing from one phase of the material to another, that the play is not continuing in naturalistic order but shifting to a new 'angle.' "[12] Clurman admires the massive gray setting of the play too, which appears real, but is "almost classically imposing, like that of an imperial mansion gone to seed and turned hollow,"[13] a description of the setting that captures the play's themes and atmosphere and is suggestive of the profound action that the play reveals.

The Homecoming is not the only play, however, in which

reviewers have detected production elements that convey those depths that lie below the naturalistic surface. Miss Kemp-Welch's television production of *Birthday Party* was considered masterly by a critic in the *Daily Mail* because her use of "natural and stylized techniques mostly in swiftly inter-cut close-ups, clarified the individual dialogue and created a menacing atmosphere of unreality,—just what was needed."[14] The film of *The Servant* was praised for its "emphasis given to angles and staircases" which the reviewer suggests were used "as a latent symbolism of the complex moral ascendancies and submissions which work as interdependently as the water-levels in a chain of canal locks."[15] And *The Accident* was admired for a technique that gives proper emphasis to the Pinter undercurrents. "But the characters refuse to be limited by what we are shown of them. The whole film is put together virtually without transitions, using only direct cuts, and as with Resnais, it is in the gaps that the real story is told."[16]

One can only conclude, I think, that very often the intuitive playing of the drama's reality allows the undercurrents of poetry and ritual to emerge—for emerge they do in production. When seeing a rerun of Miss Kemp-Welch's television production of *The Lover*, I was struck by the effect one gets of the sex war that emerges from the sex games. The rhythms of the lines along with the use of the drum underscore the ritual content of the piece; and one is faced not so much with realistic lovers as with a ritual of love that is in danger of losing its significance, but receives new life in the course of the play.

Returning to Pinter's direction of *The Man in the Glass Booth*, one may find important clues to a desirable production style for his own plays. Like his own drama, the play has elements of mystery and melodrama transmuted into the realm of ritual and myth—a transmutation beautifully realized on stage.

The critical reaction to the Shaw drama and production

seemed to fall into a kind of confusion not unlike the critical response to Pinter's *Birthday Party* or *Homecoming*. Irving Wardle criticized it as an "over-ambitious melodrama" that hangs on the question of whether the wealthy Jew Arthur Goldman "is a war criminal, or whether he is masquerading as one." He found Pinter's direction "painfully slow," doing "nothing to conceal the inertia of the supporting parts or the childish improbability of the trial scene."[17] W. A. Darlington, who found the play more interesting than Wardle did, was baffled by it and made no attempt to answer either question that he thought the play posed. Is Goldman the war criminal Dorf, and if so, why does he pretend to be Jewish; or if he is Jewish, why does he pretend to be Dorf?[18]

Harold Hobson, an early defender of Pinter's *Birthday Party*, also was able to make some sense of the Shaw play, which he correctly pointed out will be misread if taken as melodrama. The play is about the difficulty of forgiveness, as Hobson sees it, with Goldman enacting the role of an ironical Christ figure, "taking on his own shoulders the sins of other men, not so that they may be washed clean, but in order that the men who committed them may be rendered eternally hateful."[19] Walter Kerr's criticism of the play also stressed the danger of accepting the play as melodrama or naturalism alone, and suggested that "the author is teasing us rather than putting a real man together."[20] Kerr's attempt to solve the play's riddle on a purely symbolic plane, however, falls curiously flat and makes it easier to understand Pinter's impatience with approaches to his own plays as parable, symbol, or allegory.

Perhaps Kerr might have avoided an oversimplified explanation of the play as anti-Christian and anti-martyr[21] if he had not insisted on the drama as parable rather than reality. Surely it is both. The author is not merely teasing us with ideas but is placing a very real man before us and allowing him and his situation to suggest far more than he or any character in the play explains. I think it is fairly clear that the richness of texture and meaning that emerges both from *The Man in the Glass Booth* and Pinter's plays derives from an insistence by the authors upon the concrete and upon the reality of their vision, whatever symbolic implications are present.

Still Kerr's suggestion that the staging of the play tended to underline the symbolic and ritualistic nature of the drama[22] is entirely valid. When I pointed this out to the actor in the play, Lawrence Pressman, and suggested to him as well that the acting in the play seemed highly theatrical and unrealistic at times, Pressman insisted that the style was at most a heightened realism. It grew, he said, out of the reality of the text, which had to be believed in an imaginative way. I would agree that Pinter as director took his stylistic cues from the play, but there is no doubt that his direction helped to bring out the symbolic as well as the realistic nature of the script. The play's ritual opening complete with Buddha-like praying figure and Verdi Requiem gave the cumulative impression of a Catholic mass, and the Christ-like role of Goldman's character was heightened by the staging of his arrest and the stripping of him on stage. Working both realistically and symbolically, Pinter's direction made very clear an ambiguity in man's struggle for power and for salvation.

The somewhat surrealistic, bizarre setting and staging of the piece not only reflect the bizarre character of Goldman, but also reflect at least an intuitive grasp on Pinter's part of the play as parable as well as reality. The blond and red-headed Israelites in the play are clearly another version of the Hitler youth movement, and Goldman's autocratic behavior with his underlings is a cross between a kind of Hitler and a sentimental gangland boss. Pleasence's intensely human, agonized portrayal of a vindictive and forgiving man, who makes love to his prosecutor and lashes out at his fellow-sufferers, who can hardly forgive himself for being alive and for loving life, and who locks himself in his glass booth both defeated and victorious, is juxtaposed with the clear voice of Sonia Dresdel, who plays the woman who exposes his masquerade. The Jews, she cries, in answer to his assertion that they too would have followed Hitler if chosen, would not have followed where he led. The woman, however, embraces the man she exposes, and as she reaches out to him so does the audience, trying to understand in this suffering and violent human being the nature of all men who cannot accept the evil in life but who nevertheless continue to love and hate.

Pinter's ability to bring out the real and symbolic movement of the piece was apparently more than intuitive. He had taken Pressman to a pub one afternoon and discussed his film *The Servant* with him, pointing out the love-hate relationship in the film as well as in all master-servant relationships. Pressman, as Goldman's secretarial hireling in the play, was apparently missing the hate, the undercurrent of "back-hall talk of servants." Pressman claimed that this talk with Pinter gave him the clue to an overall outlook that helped him play the cell scene with Goldman in the second act. At this point Pressman remarked too on the fact that Pinter has said that all of his plays are about the question of dominance, which is one reason, perhaps, for his attraction to the Shaw play.

Pinter never lost track of *The Man in the Glass Booth* as he had first defined it to his cast as a play about "a Jew who pretends to be a Nazi but is really a Jew." In finding the humanity of Goldman on stage, though, he found ways as well to portray Goldman's action as a search for the redemption of himself and mankind. The heightened realism he employed as director included those specific rituals that the text suggested and that emerged on stage as both real and symbolic, so that the audience viewed "Goldman" in the glass booth and "the man" in the glass booth. Such heightened realism, often bordering on the surrealistic in this production, seems to me to be an ideal approach to Pinter's own plays in production. I cannot imagine either that an awareness of the ritual nature of the action in Pinter's drama could be anything but helpful to the director who held on as well to the individual reality of that action, or that an awareness of the nature of his characters as archetype and individual need inhibit the actor if he holds on to the character as individual.

If Pinter's direction of *The Man in the Glass Booth* offers clues to a desirable production style for Pinter's plays, I do not feel as reluctant as some of Pinter's current directors to suggest that that style is a distinctive one. I share their regard for the value of intuition in acting and directing and am aware of the dangers in over-intellectualizing or concentrating on symbols. But when the texts of the plays have so consistently revealed a ritual base, to ignore their ritual counterpoint in production would seem to me to be missing that reality upon which the plays are based. In the light of a ritual reading, *The Homecoming* set, more surrealistic than naturalistic, is suggestive of the dreamlike and ritual plane of action which develops in the play. The pauses in the plays are specifically related to the characters' gradual movement toward the sacrificial rites in which they are involved. The "wasp" episode in *A Slight Ache* would suffer in production if the actors playing Flora and Edward did not regard the wasp as real; but if the actor playing Edward is asked to sacrifice the wasp rather than merely to kill it, the humor and tragedy of the wasp scene may serve as a proper prelude to the larger sacrifice of Edward that the play is about. Certainly the ritual elements in the production of *The Man in the Glass Booth* were quite consciously enhanced by Pinter's direction of that play.

When I suggested to Pinter, however, at a chance meeting with him that this production had cleared up many of my questions about a desirable production style for his plays, he smiled. It had not, he assured me, cleared up his questions.[23]

Conclusion

*"I desire a mysterious art, always reminding
and half reminding those who understand it of dearly
loved things, doing its work by suggestion, not by
direct statement, a complexity of rhythm, colour,
gesture, not space pervading like the intellect but
a memory and a prophecy."*[1]

Even though Pinter, contrary to Yeats, does not desire a "mysterious art," he has, nevertheless, achieved it. The mysterious and prophetic quality of his drama results, though, from an almost scientific attempt at dispassionate observation. When asked if he tried to make Barrett a sympathetic character in his film version of *The Servant*, Pinter did not consider such a task his concern. He said, "I am just concerned with what people are, with accuracy."[2]

Pinter's preoccupation with accuracy is related to his desire for precision and economy. The precise gesture, the precise sound, the precise word are all part of his poetic technique, in which a word too many may destroy the desired effect. Despite the intuitive nature of his work, Pinter chisels away at his creations like a Greek sculptor until they have the simplicity and accuracy of line that will make his statement exact. When discussing the difference in writing for the cinema and the stage, Pinter agreed that they were different media that made different demands; but he found the same need for discipline and economy in both. Speaking of the cinema, he says:

> I know that you can get *around* a hell of a lot more—there's no comparison there—but the disciplines are similar, for a writer, in that although you need, let's say, less words on the screen than you do on the stage, nevertheless—although I don't really believe this to be true—say that you needed twenty words for a particular scene on the stage, you can do with six for a similar scene on the screen. The point is, that if you write eight for the screen, two words too many, you're overloading the thing, and you're breaking your discipline; precisely the same discipline, the same economy, whatever the medium you're writing for.[3]

Pinter's own experiences as an actor and director with radio, television, stage, and screen have doubtless contributed to his understanding of the economy necessary for each medium and for his unusual mastery of such a variety of forms. Despite his achievements, however, in the various entertainment media of our time, Pinter finds the theater "ultimately the most important medium,"[4] and he has suggested that he reserves his most important ideas for the stage.[5] He finds writing for the theater the most difficult, the most restricted, "the most naked kind" of writing because "you're just *there*, stuck—there are your characters stuck on the stage, you've got to live with them and deal with them."[6] All of Pinter's dramatic world exhibits something of this quality of dealing with life accurately and revealing it in its naked truth.

In dealing with his characters so accurately, Pinter has looked far beneath the surface of life, not only to the psychological depths of his characters' existence, but to their primitive archetypal nature. His characters and the actions of his plays remain mysterious, not because he withholds psychological explanation, but because he has sensed a deeper strand of reality than the particular psychology of a character. This other reality is of a ritual nature, the characters grouping to enact those ancient rites that imitate nature and insure and celebrate life's persistence and renewal.

Ritual functions in Pinter's dramatic world much as Jane Ellen Harrison suggests it functions in religion to keep the individual fenced-in soul open—"to other souls, other separate lives, and to the apprehension of other forms of life."[7] The daily rituals that protect man from such openness and awareness are constantly undermined in Pinter's dramas by those sacrificial rites that impinge upon them and force contact. Goldberg and McCann disturb the breakfast rituals of *The Birthday Party* to conduct their own ritual party at which Stanley is sacrificed; and Petey can no longer hide behind his paper when the strips of it which McCann has torn during the party fall out to remind him of Stanley's victimization. In *The Room* Rose can no longer hide behind her ritual breakfasts with her husband when Riley appears from the basement and involves her in his fate as *pharmakos*. As much as his characters evade communication, Pinter involves them in an eventual confrontation. The structure is Aristotelian, the imitation of an action, and the impact of the characters upon one another, even in their silent exchanges, is as final and irrevocable as the impact of character on character in Greek tragedy.

The Golden Bough kings have served in this exploration of Pinter's dramatic world as a metaphorical clue to the ritual patterns that form the basis of it. The contests for dominance which are at the center of the dramatic action of each play invariably have been fought with the tenacity of those priests who defended the Golden Bough with their lives. The battles have also taken on the symbolic significance of seasonal change and renewal attached to the

Golden Bough ritual by Frazer and the Cambridge school of anthropology. In the seasonal ritual the old king-priest-god invariably must suffer death or banishment (Davies, Teddy, Edward—all must be sacrificed), either to be re-born as the new spirit of spring and life (Edward becomes the matchseller, Stanley becomes the new creation of Monty and Co.) or to be replaced by a new god (Teddy is replaced by Lenny and Joey, Law is replaced by Stott, Davies loses the battle to the young gods already in pos-session, Mick and Aston). The role played by Pinter's women is also clearer if their place as fertility goddess in the ritual is understood: Flora's welcome of the match-seller as her new mate and Ruth's adoption of her new household both make ritual sense of what on the surface seem sluttish and irrational choices. The new god must re-ceive a welcome and be joined with mother earth if life is to continue.

The seasonal nature of the ritual is most clearly exhibited in the one-act drama *A Slight Ache* in which Edward's sacrifice is viewed in the context of a garden. As the dying god of winter, Edward has lost touch with his garden and with his wife, Flora, whose name and character reveal her close connection with the garden. The beautiful summer weather is frightening to Edward, who is happy for a moment only when he kills "the first wasp of summer." This sacrificial act is a prelude to his own sacrifice, how-ever, as the new god, the matchseller who haunts his home, replaces him in it. Flora recognizes the matchseller as Barnabas, the god of summer, and embraces him as the new god in her role as fertility goddess.

In the ritual patterning of the plays, Pinter envisions his characters, like the priests of Nemi, as victors as well as victims. In his early plays his victim-victors are menaced by an outside force, messengers of Monty in *The Birthday Party* or a voice that speaks for Wilson in *The Dumb Waiter*; and whatever brief victories their lives afford, the impression of the plays is mainly one of man as victim. Beginning with *A Slight Ache*, however, the menace is internalized, and man is seen rather as the victim of forces within himself (the matchseller is another part of Edward) than as victim of some larger exterior power. As the plays gain in complexity, the role of the victim-victor is complicated until Ruth in *The Homecoming* is seen as both the suffering sacrificial victim and the ruling fertility goddess, victim and victor at one and the same time. Pinter conceives of life as a battleground on which there is no clear-cut victory or defeat, always victory and defeat; a battleground on which the enemy, who often seems distant and distinct, is often but another aspect of the self.

The battleground becomes as significant as the battle for dominance in much of Pinter's dramatic world and gains the symbolic value of the tree bearing the Golden Bough so rigorously guarded by its priests. We see Len in *The Dwarfs* trying to integrate the elements of his room and himself, to rid his "kingdom" of the dwarfs who inhabit it; Davies in *The Caretaker* trying to wrest the haven from Aston that his benefactor would share with him; Stott and Law in *The Basement* alternately possessing the basement apartment for which they vie; and Barrett in the film *The Servant* imposing his personality on the house as well as its master. Place is a haven in which Rose and Stanley hide in *The Room* and *The Birthday Party*; it is the focus of the dreams and aspirations of Aston, Mick, and Davies in *The Caretaker*; and it is haven, prison, and castle for Ruth in *The Homecoming*. The self is at stake in Pinter's dramatic portrayal of his victim-victors battling for a place that is identified with that self and that must be guarded, defended, or taken rather than shared.

The struggle in the dramas is very often conceived of in Oedipal terms. Father-and-son competition is evident in Pinter's three major plays with the mother-wife the focus of the battle in *The Homecoming*. The sexual relationship is ritualized, however, so that the focus is not on neurotic relationships or Oedipus complexes so much as it is on the archetypal relationships of man and woman faced with the universal dilemma of Oedipal conflicts. Woman is often seen in these conflicts as mother, wife and whore—the over-possessive mother of *A Night Out*, for example, whom Albert identifies with a whore he picks up on the street. In *Tea Party* women are initially divided as wife and secretary (whore), but by the end of the play the dying Disson sees them both as one and the same, whores catering to his usurping brother-in-law.

In *The Lover, The Collection,* and *The Homecoming*—plays that make a similar identification of the woman—Pinter is highly sympathetic with them. This sympathetic treatment seems to stem partly from a perception of the woman's ritual role in the transfer of power from the dying god to the new god. Woman is not allowed the role of faithful wife if she is to preside at the ritual renewal of life and embrace and welcome the new god when he arrives. Ruth, the most complex of these divided women, is portrayed as the suffering victim of the power struggle that she loses and wins, the fertility goddess who says "yes" to life on whatever harsh terms it is offered.

The dramas move, then, beyond the particular psychological attributes of the battling characters to their archetypal roles in the ritual patterns in which they move. Pinter once remarked in an interview that a sameness of behavior "is rife in the world. As someone said 'we're all the same upside down.' "[8] In a sense his dramatic world stresses that sameness as well as the patterns in which we all appear to move.

One might conclude, then, that despite the different disguises of the menace in each Pinter play, the same weasel is always hiding under the cocktail cabinet. Such a conclusion must be qualified, however, because there is much more to a Pinter play than its ritual pattern. Pinter's close and exact look at modern man, and particular English men, is what opens out into his intuitive grasp of the basic and primitive rhythms that have always moved men. The ritual counterpoint, the interweaving of the daily secular rituals of modern life with the sacrificial rites at the plays' centers, is what creates the texture of Pinter's dramatic world rather than the sacrificial rites alone. Ruth serves the family tea before she gives herself. And the giving of herself has its particular tragi-comic power because the primitive action takes place in a living room, in the understated tones of a modern business deal amidst cups and saucers rather than in a primitive or heroic setting. The weasels are many as well as one, and the way they work, the particular illusive forms they take, contributes to the particular meaning of each play.

Hence, Pinter continually responds to the texture of modern life as well as to the forces that have always given pattern to life. In *The Birthday Party* Goldberg is almost a caricature of the contemporary corrupted businessman whose middle-class values are a mask for the brutal forces he embodies and serves. In *The Caretaker* Davies is a more fully rounded portrait of the dispossessed vagrant of modern cities. His portrait is completed by the depiction of the equally restless Mick and the wounded Aston, whose efforts to fix a plug become symbolic of his efforts to integrate himself and offer a potent comment on the fragmented nature of city life today. And Max, the uncertain and eventually unseated patriarch of *The Homecoming*, the ex-butcher who has fathered a pimp, a demolition worker, and a professor, stands as the father of a world whose civilization is corrupt (Lenny), brutal (Joey), and effete (Teddy). *The Homecoming* depicts the struggle within the family unit for salvation, as Max, Lenny, and Joey reach out to Ruth for whatever grace she can offer, and the "intellectual" Teddy relinquishes the struggle even as he has relinquished life itself.

The struggle for salvation in our modern world is perhaps Pinter's major theme, even as it is the theme of so much of modern literature and drama. His vision a tragicomic one, Pinter often laughs at the absurdities of the struggle, often sympathizes with the suffering that it entails. His focus ranges in his plays, settling now on the dying Edward with his growing self-knowledge in *A Slight Ache*, now on the conquering Stephen with his anguished sense of victory in *The Accident*, now on the victim-victor Ruth who comes home to serve and to rule. At one minute his satirical eye moves toward parody, as Stanley becomes almost a mock scapegoat of the malignant powers who reign; but his sense of involvement continually tips the scale with a sympathetic awareness of the suffering involved, in this case the suffering of McCann and Goldberg as well as Stanley.

Despite its accuracy, then, Pinter's dramatic world is anything but the cold and clinical creation of a scientific observer. When Hayman wrongly identifies Pinter with his own character in *The Homecoming*, Teddy,[9] he places him with the only evil character Pinter has created, the already dead person who refuses to become involved in life because life itself is outside his province. Despite the terrible protest against society and against certain qualities of modern life that Pinter's plays contain, he never detaches himself and satirizes that life as a problem. He rather merges with his characters and shares their feeling of being menaced. Hence, we too as the audience are menaced and experience the plays with all the suspense of living through an ordeal. His plays become an initiation for us—an experiencing of the death in our culture from which we may emerge with a clearer insight and some feeling of renewal.

Pinter, in fact, not only uncovers the primitive rhythms which lie below the surface of civilization, but also explores the celebration which accompanies the most cruel rituals of life. Euripides' play *The Bacchae* serves as an excellent clue to the nature of Pinter's celebration: a play in which one aspect of man, the civilized, repressed side (Pentheus), is destroyed only to emerge once his dismembered body is put back together again in the epiphany as the god Dionysus, the primitive god of fertility whose power must be recognized. If Stanley's projected reincarnation in the image of Monty in *The Birthday Party* is too brutal for celebration, the matchseller who replaces Edward in *A Slight Ache* does emerge, ironical though his appearance, as the bringer of new life; and the family to whom Ruth returns in *The Homecoming* is vitally, brutally alive in comparison with her banished husband.

And if the power of the emerging god must be recognized, that recognition comes in Pinter's drama to the dying god figure as well as to the audience. Echoes of the rhythms of *Oedipus Rex* enter the plays as the insights of Pinter's characters are often accompanied by a loss of sight. Stanley is robbed of his glasses and forced into a game of blind man's bluff at his birthday party; his eyes are painfully opened to the nightmare situation of his life with which he cannot cope. Edward and Disson both suffer blindness, a retreat from their growing insights. In Pinter's dramas, the dying god has at least an intuitive recognition of both his plight and himself.

The celebration in Pinter's dramas, though, is tempered by the nature of his victorious figures. Like Yeats, Pinter speculates fearfully on the nature of the new gods. The passive, stinking matchseller of *A Slight Ache*, the brutal brothers of *The Homecoming*, the conniving brother-in-law of *Tea Party* do not suggest all that is most welcome in spring. In Ionesco's dramatic world, there is no salvation; in Beckett's, there is a seeking for salvation; and in Pinter's, the salvation which does arrive comes in such questionable form that it is hard to accept. Pinter's drama remains enigmatic and mysterious then, even as its ritual rhythms celebrate the continual renewal of life.

But if the heart of the mystery to Pinter is as comic as it is tragic, perhaps his laughter contains a mysterious renewal beyond the one depicted. Christopher Fry suggests that in comedy, "groaning as we may be, we move in the figure of a dance, and, so moving we trace the outline of the mystery."[10] Pinter's dance may be macabre, but its rhythms go back to the mainstream of drama; and even if his mockery of the ritual he employs poses a haunting question for man, its rhythms suggest a kind of answer as well.

Epilogue: Beyond Menace

"I felt that after The Homecoming, . . . *I couldn't any longer stay in the room with this bunch of people who opened doors and came in and went out.* Landscape *and* Silence *are in a very different form. There isn't any menace at all."*[1]

Pinter's one-act plays, *Landscape* (1968) and *Silence* (1969), and his short dramatic sketch *Night* (presented in *Mixed Doubles* in 1969), indicate a somewhat new direction for the playwright. He himself puts his finger on the major change when he mentions their lack of menace.[2] In production as a double bill at the Aldwich Theater in 1969, *Landscape* and *Silence* lacked physical action as well. In *Landscape*, originally performed on radio, a middle-aged couple, Beth and Duff, sit and speak at a kitchen table. In *Silence* Ellen, Rumsey, and Bates sit in three even less clearly defined areas and speak.

Gone is the sacrifice of a scapegoat at the center of so many of Pinter's dramas. No exchange of power, no outer conflict or exterior confrontation shapes the drama. To say that the characters converse is even inexact; in *Landscape* the man addresses the woman, but he does not appear to hear her, and the woman neither addresses the man nor appears to hear him. Direct exchanges take place in *Silence*, but they are brief; and the technique of *Landscape*, that of interweaving of streams of consciousness, predominates. As the action moves inward (nothing happens, but much is explored), one is reminded of the dramatic experiments of O'Neill's *Strange Interlude* or of the sometimes half-conscious exchanges in Maeterlinck's *Pelléas et Mélisande*. The revelation of private thoughts, experiences, dreams, rejections—often only partly conscious—reveals the strong influence too of Joyce, Proust, Woolf, and the more recent Robbe-Grillet, as Pinter borrows and transmutes the novelists' techniques for his own experiments with forms of poetic drama.

The dramas retain from the playwright's previous work, however, not only a concern with the same themes and kinds of relationships but also the rhythms of ritual. The absence of physically active dramatic confrontation and sacrifice precludes the full cyclic rhythms of his other work, but the poetic counterpoint of these more recent plays gains much of its dramatic impetus not only from the balanced opposition of the interior dreams and private personalities of the characters but also from a ritualistic treatment of time (see pp. 38-39).

In *Landscape*, Beth's lines are an incantation to a past experience of love fulfilled. For her the kitchen in which she sits does not seem to exist as her wish to capture past experience brings its setting into the present and extends it into the future. Once in her life she had experienced a complete fulfillment. Is it forever lost in her life with her dull husband Duff?

> BETH: I would like to stand by the sea. It is there.
> *Pause.*
> I have. Many times. It's something I cared for. I've done it.
> *Pause.*

I'll stand on the beach. On the beach. Well . . . it was very fresh. But it was hot, in the dunes. But it was so fresh, on the shore. I loved it very much. (P. 9)

The three tenses used at the play's opening define time as it exists for Beth. Because she cared about her experience of love on the beach, it has become the only reality which exists for her. The sea is there for her, it was there, she wishes it to be there, and in her private world she will still stand by it.

Beth re-creates the archetypal reality of her past as a bulwark against the present reality of her husband, whom she neither sees nor hears. Against the yearningly domestic picture of her which her husband paints—that of a good housekeeper and servant and a good wife, who can forgive him his infidelities with a kiss—is her picture of herself as a beautiful, childbearing, flower-watering, adored woman —in fact, a goddess. Her removal from the daily reality that concerns her husband reinforces Beth's role as the familiar fertility goddess figure from Pinter's dramatic world (especially the heroine of A Slight Ache), the wife-whore-mother, but one who differs from his earlier heroines in her lack of inner conflict over the roles. Beth has come to accept the inevitability of her present frustrations (not even a matchseller hovers at the back gate), but she does so only by lingering on the archetypal reality of her past experience by the water. Aphrodite, a goddess born of the sea, is a significant mythical reference for Ruth in The Homecoming as well as for Beth in this play.

The conflict emerges, rather, and is enriched in the attempts of Duff to make contact with Beth, attempts which fail but grow in intensity as she relives her past experience. Beth is so enthralled with the remembered light touch of her lover that the heavy-handed crudeness of Duff is unable to reach her at all. His concentration on daily existence, his walk to the pond, his discourses on the proper manufacture of beer to display his expertise and superiority, and his pride in his domestic abilities, take on something of the ridiculous in the light of her indifference and preoccupation. Duff's efforts to reach Beth, however, reveal a wistful intuition of the greater validity of her experience compared with his own. He dwells on his domestic abilities—"I could drive well, I could polish his shoes well, I earned my keep" (p. 20)—and likes to think they have been a good domestic "team"; but he also paints a picture of himself as isolated—unable, for example, to enter the joke of children he met or to share his wife's vision, a vision which includes children.

> BETH: The dog sat down by me. I stroked him. Through the window I could see down into the valley. I saw children in the valley. They were running through the grass. They ran up the hill.
> *Long Silence.*
> DUFF: I never saw your face. You were standing by the windows. One of those black nights. A downfall. All I could hear was the rain on the glass, smacking on the glass. You knew I'd come in but you didn't move. I stood close to you. What were you looking at? . . . (P. 27)

Tension subtly increases as Duff's inability to make contact does. That tension finally erupts into Duff's fantasy of violence and rape, a fantasy ironically juxtaposed with Beth's gentle memory of fulfillment.

> DUFF: I took the chain off and the thimble, the keys, the scissors slid off it and clattered down. I booted the gong down the hall. The dog came in. I thought you would come to me, I thought you would come into my arms and kiss me, even . . . offer yourself to me. I would have had you in front of the dog, like a man, in the hall, on the stone, banging the gong, mind you don't get the scissors up your arse, or the thimble, don't worry, I'll throw them for the dog to chase, the thimble will keep the dog happy, he'll play with it with his paws, you'll plead with me like a woman, I'll bang the gong on the floor, if the sound is too flat, lacks, resonance, I'll hang it back on its hook, bang you against it swinging, gonging, waking the place up,

calling them all for dinner, lunch is up, bring out the bacon, bang your lovely head, mind the dog doesn't swallow the thimble, slam—

BETH: He lay above me and looked down at me. He supported my shoulder.

Pause.

So tender his touch on my neck. So softly his kiss on my cheek. (P. 29)

Duff's confessed infidelity working in counterpoint with Beth's unconfessed, but re-created, infidelity is the central irony of the piece, while Duff's attempts to make contact in his own crude, dull, unimaginative way with the deeper reality which he senses Beth embodies is its central dramatic focus. The final counterpoint of fantasy in rape (Duff) and love fulfilled (Beth) remains dramatic as Duff's anger reflects his failure to make contact, and Beth's sense of transcendent, mythical time makes her isolation, paradoxically, a connection. Rather than an archetypal reality emerging into the daily lives of the people (*The Homecoming, A Slight Ache*), all remains muted, essentially unexpressed, contained only in the fantasies of the characters. For Duff, frustration passionately felt, for Beth reality only in a dream.

Silence is perhaps even more complex than *Landscape* in its musical counterpoint and is touched with a more vibrant affirmation. Movement is both the topic and effect of this seemingly static play as the thoughts of the three characters intertwine in a veritable dance. Even while the difficulties of connection are discussed, the problems of seeing and hearing, at least two of the characters transcend those difficulties while the discordant notes of the third are essential to the drama's musical harmony.

Again the themes are of love and time. The triangle of earlier Pinter plays makes up the plot as Ellen and her two men, Rumsey and Bates, reflect on life and Ellen has a brief interchange with each. Replacing the earlier dramas' competition over women (the cyclic interchange of *The Basement, A Slight Ache,* or *The Homecoming*), in which the insurance of life involves change of partner, and, going beyond *Landscape,* in which cyclic interchange is alive as a memory and a bulwark against the present, *Silence* reveals the triangle in equipoise. The play might be a sequel to *The Homecoming* in which we see Ruth in a variety of roles giving life to various men and finding her life through them.

In many ways *Silence* is as still as the tableau at the end of that play, and yet as filled with life, movement, and questions. Will Ruth kiss the aging father? How will she deal with the brutalities of the men, find sustenance of love or power? *Silence* gives a glimmering insight into the archetypal stasis to which *The Homecoming* moves.

Late in the brief play, Ellen reflects on the unreality of the people about her.

> After my work each day I walk back through people but I don't notice them. I'm not in a dream or anything of that sort. On the contrary. I'm quite wide awake to the world around me. But not to the people. There must be something in them to notice, to pay attention to, something of interest in them. In fact I know there is . . . I'm certain of it. But I pass through them noticing nothing. It is only later, in my room, that I remember. Yes, I remember. But I'm never sure that what I remember is of to-day or of yesterday or of a long time ago.
>
> And then often it is only half things I remember, half things, beginnings of things. (P. 46)

The first part of the play develops some of the memories of the three characters and some interchanges between Ellen and each of the men, while the last few pages which follow the remark are echoes, fragments, "half things" from what has gone before. The reality of time, of mythical sacred time, no longer lies in the past remembered as opposed to the present (*Landscape*) or in the past made present (the rebirth of Ruth as Jessie in *The Homecom-*

ing.) It lies, rather, in a counterpoint of memories, a juxtaposition of insights, a flow of experience which is ever illusive, but ever significant.

Rumsey is a walker in the country, sensitive to the landscape, the animals, the textures of life and light. He can love and listen, and therefore he can also let go.

> I tell her my life's thoughts, clouds racing. She looks up at me
> or listens looking down. She stops in midsentence, my sentence, to look up at me. Sometimes her hand has slipped from
> mine, her arm loosened, she walks slightly apart, dog barks.
> (P. 33)

Bates, on the other hand, is a rider of buses to the city, restless, unsatisfied and grasping in his relationships, like Duff desperate for a love he cannot achieve.

> Caught a bus to the town. Crowds, lights round the market,
> rain and stinking. Showed her the bumping lights. Took her
> down around the dumps. Black roads and girders. She clutching me. This way the way I bring you. Pubs throw the doors
> smack into the night. Cars barking and the lights. She with
> me, clutching. (P. 34)

The peace of Rumsey, "pleasant alone and watch the folding light" (p. 35), is juxtaposed with the frenzy of Bates, "I'm at my last gasp with this unendurable racket" (p. 35).

All three characters speak of their great age, though they are in their twenties (Ellen), thirties (Bates), and forties (Rumsey), respectively. The two men are each old enough to know—or begin to know—what and who they are. Ellen clearly is not—indeed, she is just beginning to speculate about such problems. Rumsey tells Ellen to seek a young man but she refuses. Bates speaks of having experienced all things in the somewhat world-weary tones of Eliot's Prufrock, though he is for more resentful; and Ellen wonders about aging even as she wonders about whether she thinks or what she is. Though young, all three suffer from a sense that secular time is passing them by, leaving them behind, undefined.

Sacred time, however, does not completely elude the three and is worked out in terms of vision. Bates remembers walking with a child (Ellen perhaps) who saw a shape or shadow in a tree which he identified for her as a resting bird. Later in the play he assumes the child's vision. "I see something in a tree, a shape, a shadow" (p. 48). Beset by city lights, Bates wonders if he could change his life and live by night. "What can be meant by living in the dark?" (p. 36). He feels imprisoned by his environment, by himself: "I walk in my mind. But can't get out of the walls, into a wind. Meadows are walled, and lakes. The sky's a wall" (pp. 39-40). His later child's vision of a shape, a shadow, is suggestive of some small breakthrough into the darkness, though his final rejection of love, "Sleep? Tender Love? It's of no importance" (p. 51), seems to rob him of any sustained breakthrough into the light.

Light is constantly associated with vision but tends to take place in darkness. Ellen wonders if it is darker as one goes up higher. It is in the night and the silence that she reflects on her age and her existence. Ellen, however, walks in the wind that excludes Bates. "I go up with the milk. The sky hits me. I walk in the wind to collide with them waiting" (p. 45). She also sees lights in the distance of the black landscape and has an overcertain memory of her wedding which makes it as illusive as the lights.

Rumsey, more at peace than either Ellen or Bates, cares for his horses, cares for his women, but he wonders if contact can be made.

> I shall walk down to my horse and see how my horse is. He'll come towards me. Perhaps he doesn't need me, my visit, my care, will be like any other visit, any other care. I can't believe it. (P. 39)

A juxtaposition of lines which suggest sexual union between Rumsey and Ellen and transcendent insight for

Ellen is followed by a statement on the illusiveness of vision and life by Rumsey.

> ELLEN: When I run . . . when I run . . . when I run . . . over the grass . . .
> RUMSEY: She floats . . . under me. Floating . . . under me.
> ELLEN: I turn. I turn. I wheel. I glide. I wheel. In stunning light. The horizon moves from the sun. I am crushed by the light.
> *Silence.*
> RUMSEY: Sometimes I see people. They walk towards me, no, not so, walk in my direction, but never reaching me, turning left, or disappearing, and then reappearing, to disappear into the wood. So many ways to lose sight of them, then to recapture sight of them. They are sharp at first sight . . . then smudged . . . then lost . . . then glimpsed again . . . then gone.
> BATES: Funny. Sometimes I press my hand on my forehead, calmingly, feel all the dust drain out, let it go, feel the grit slip away. Funny moment. That calm moment. (Pp. 40-41)

The statement of calm from Bates becomes a comment on Rumsey's experience, almost as if Bates and Rumsey are different aspects of one man. Despite the illusiveness of life, the calm moment exists.

The participation of the senses in the movement of time is what tends to define it. Ellen is crushed by lightness, or it evades her. Sight and sound interweave as the three seek connection.

> RUMSEY: She was looking down. I couldn't hear what she said.
> BATES: I can't hear you. Yes you can, I said.
> RUMSEY: What are you saying? Look at me, she said.
> BATES: I didn't. I didn't hear you, she said. I didn't hear what you said.
> RUMSEY: But I am looking at you. It's your head that's bent.
> *Silence* (Pp. 43-44)

If contact is made only briefly, intermittently, tenuously —if the memory of marriage or union is itself uncertain for

Ellen, the effort of living an ordeal for Bates with "not even any damn inconstant solace" (p. 36), the uncertainty of response a constant awareness for Rumsey, "But I am looking at you. It's your head that's bent" (p. 44)—still the thoughts and actions do suggest an interaction. Despite its stasis, the drama contains a tremendous sense of life: the three characters move in their uncertain relationships, their thoughts and desires unresolved, but present; if not a veritable hymn to life, there is at least the suggestion of possibilities. Ellen and Rumsey have some degree of mutual understanding, and even Bates may grow in comprehension.

The hymn is fully sung in the slight dramatic sketch, *Night*, in which husband and wife reminisce amusingly over their meeting—each remembering it differently—and then reminisce over their reminiscences as if they too are in the past.

> WOMAN: And then we had children and we sat and talked and you remembered women on bridges and towpaths and rubbish dumps.
>
> MAN: And you remembered your bottom against railings and men holding your hands and men looking into your eyes.
>
> WOMAN: And talking to me softly.
>
> MAN: And your soft voice. Talking to them softly at night.
>
> WOMAN: And they said I will adore you always.
>
> MAN: Saying I will adore you always. (P. 61)

As the past is carried into the present and memories merge, they include other men and other women in a flow of love. The present—the need to get up early the next morning—becomes part of a general flow of life and love in which the couple merge, ironically, but still with fullness, with understanding, and with delight.

The order of publication of the three plays, all on the subject of love, would appear to be significant. In *Land-*

scape the affirmation of love remembered is qualified by the couple's lack of communication as Duff is left wistfully and angrily forever outside of contact with his wife and her reality. Although in *Silence* Bates would seem to be rejected by Ellen in favor of Rumsey, he is no longer seen as the outsider in the fashion of Duff so much as he is considered in opposition to Rumsey. The triangle is alive with life on stage; the past is still alive in the present and is open to the flow of the future. The physicality of Bates is seen in balance with the gentler and wiser understanding of Rumsey through whom, by way of Ellen, Bates can somehow share in a moment of calm. And as comic as the interchange is in *Night*, the triangle has become a couple; Bates has merged with Rumsey to become a Man whom a Woman can love and accept. The wedding, so uncertain to Ellen, is present in the darkness of *Night*.

In *Landscape, Silence,* and *Night*, Pinter's earlier celebration of life's renewal, at whatever cost, is replaced by an evocation of life's flow through the mind and through time. The ironies remain, the questions vibrate, but the celebration persists and grows.

NOTES

Preface

1. "Two People in a Room," in "Talk of the Town," *New Yorker,* 25 February 1967, p. 25.

2. "Pinterism Is Maximum Tension through Minimum Information," *New York Times,* 1 October 1967, p. 89.

3. Quoted by Kathleen Halton, "Pinter," *Vogue,* 1 October 1964, p. 246.

4. "Two People in a Room," p. 36.

5. Ibid., pp. 35-36.

6. Quoted by Julian Holland, "The No. 296 All-night Bus to Success . . . ," *Evening News,* 14 May 1960.

7. "Theatre," *Nation,* 23 January 1967, pp. 122-23.

Chapter I

1. Richard Y. Hathorn, *Tragedy, Myth, and Mystery,* p. 24.

2. "Writing for Myself," *Twentieth Century* 169 (February, 1961): 174.

3. Quoted by John Russell Taylor, *Anger and After,* p. 285.

4. Harold Pinter, "The Birthday Party," in *"The Birthday Party" and "The Room": Two Plays by Harold Pinter* (New York: Grove Press, Evergreen Books, 1961), p. 9. All subsequent quotations from "The Birthday Party" are from this edition.

5. Harold Pinter, "A Slight Ache," in *Three Plays by Harold Pinter* (New York: Grove Press, Evergreen Books, 1962), p. 9. All subsequent quotations from "A Slight Ache" are from this edition.

6. Quoted by Martin Esslin, *The Theatre of the Absurd,* p. 206.

7. Quoted by Roger Manvell, "The Decade of Harold Pinter," *Humanist* 132 (April, 1967): 114.

8. Esslin, *Theatre of the Absurd,* p. 199.

9. Martin Esslin, "Godot and His Children: The Theatre of Samuel

Beckett and Harold Pinter," in *Modern British Dramatists: A Collection of Critical Essays,* ed. John Russell Brown, pp. 60-63.

10. Esslin, *Theatre of the Absurd,* pp. xix-xx.

11. Walter Kerr, *Harold Pinter,* p. 3.

12. Ibid., pp. 7-20.

13. Ibid., p. 9.

14. Ibid., p. 38.

15. "Interview with Lawrence Bensky," in *Modern British Dramatists,* ed. John Russell Brown, p. 149.

16. Esslin, *Theatre of the Absurd,* p. 205.

17. Quoted by Manvell, "The Decade of Harold Pinter," p. 114.

18. Ibid.

19. Ibid.

20. Hathorn, *Tragedy, Myth and Mystery,* p. 23.

21. Ibid.

22. John Russell Brown, Introduction to *Modern British Dramatists,* pp. 10-11.

23. Hugh Nelson, *"The Homecoming:* Kith and Kinn," in *Modern British Dramatists,* ed. John Russell Brown, p. 145.

24. Harold Pinter, "The Room," in *"The Birthday Party" and "The Room": Two Plays by Harold Pinter* (New York: Grove Press, Evergreen Books, 1961), pp. 95-96. All subsequent quotations from "The Room" are from this edition.

25. Ibid., p. 155.

26. Ibid., p. 163.

27. Stanley Edgar Hyman, "The Ritual View of Myth and the Mythic," in *Myth and Literature: Contemporary Theory and Practice,* ed. John B. Vickery, p. 50.

28. David Bidney, "Myth, Symbolism, and Truth," ibid., p. 10.

29. Clyde Kluckhohn, "Myth and Ritual: A General Theory," ibid., p. 35.

30. Ibid., p. 39.

31. Ibid., pp. 43-44.

32. Bidney, "Myth, Symbolism, and Truth," p. 10.

33. Joseph Campbell, "Bias and Mythos: Prolegomena to a Science of Mythology," in *Myth and Literature,* ed. John B. Vickery, p. 19.

34. William R. Wimsatt, Jr., and Cleanth Brooks, *Literary Criticism,* p. 709.

35. Conversation with Harold Pinter, 25 August 1967, Stratford, England.

36. David R. Clark, "Metaphors for Poetry: W. B. Yeats and the Occult," in *The World of William Butler Yeats*, eds. Robin Skelton and Ann Saddlemyer, rev. ed. (Seattle: University of Washington Press, 1967), p. 38.

37. Northrop Frye, "The Archetypes of Literature," in *Myth and Literature*, ed. John B. Vickery, p. 19.

38. John B. Vickery, Introduction to *Myth and Literature*, p. ix.

39. John B. Vickery, "*The Golden Bough*: Impact and Archetype," in *Myth and Symbol: Critical Approaches and Applications*, ed. Bernice Slote, p. 196.

40. Ibid., p. 184.

41. Ibid., p. 176.

42. Ibid.

43. Ibid., p. 196.

44. Harold Pinter, "Writing for Myself," *Twentieth Century* 169 (February, 1961): 174.

Chapter 2

1. Samuel Beckett, *Waiting for Godot* (New York: Grove Press, Evergreen Books, 1964), p. 57.

2. Ibid., p. 59.

3. Sir James Frazer, *The Golden Bough*, pp. 1-2.

4. Northrop Frye, *Anatomy of Criticism*, p. 193.

5. "Excursus on the Ritual Forms Preserved in Greek Tragedy," in *Themis: A Study of the Social Origins of Greek Religion*, ed. Jane Ellen Harrison, p. 342.

6. *The Golden Bough*, p. 310.

7. Ibid., p. 313.

8. Ibid., p. 668.

9. Beckett, *Waiting for Godot*, p. 57.

10. Edward R. H. Malpas, "A Critical Analysis of the Stage Plays of Harold Pinter," p. 103.

11. Dr. Abraham N. Franzblau, quoted by Henry Hewes, "Disobedience, Civil and Uncivil," *Saturday Review*, 28 October 1967, p. 47. Copyright 1967 Saturday Review, Inc.

12. Martin Esslin, *The Theatre of the Absurd*, p. 205.

156

13. Richard Schechner, "Puzzling Pinter," *Tulane Drama Review* 11 (Winter, 1966): 178.

14. Ibid.

15. Ibid.

16. "A Critical Analysis of the Stage Plays of Harold Pinter," p. 96.

17. "Disobedience, Civil and Uncivil," *Saturday Review*, 28 October 1967, p. 47.

18. Frazer, *Golden Bough*, p. 823.

19. Eugene O'Neill, quoted by Arthur Gelb and Barbara Gelb, *O'Neill*, abr. ed. (New York: Dell Publishing Co., Laurel edition, 1965), p. 488.

20. Quoted by Arnold P. Hinchliffe, *Harold Pinter*, p. 41.

21. Personal correspondence, 28 October 1968.

22. *Myth and Reality*, p. 19.

23. Ibid.

24. "Ironic Theatre: Techniques of Irony in the Plays of Samuel Beckett, Eugene Ionesco, Harold Pinter and Jean Genet," pp. 225-26.

25. Pp. 12-14.

26. Ibid., p. 28.

27. Ibid., p. 71.

28. Ibid., p. 85.

29. Ibid., p. 90.

30. Harold Pinter, "The Dumb Waiter," in *"The Caretaker" and "The Dumb Waiter": Two Plays by Harold Pinter* (New York: Grove Press, Evergreen Books, 1961), p. 86. All subsequent quotations from "The Dumb Waiter" are from this edition.

31. *Harold Pinter*, p. 15.

32. Ibid., p. 17.

33. "A Critical Analysis of the Stage Plays of Harold Pinter," p. 167.

34. *Morning Star*, 28 February 1967.

35. Harold Pinter, "The Quiller Memorandum," film script (London: Rank Productions, 1966), p. 13. All subsequent quotations from "The Quiller Memorandum" are from this original film script.

Chapter 3

1. William Butler Yeats, "The Second Coming," in *The Collected Poems of W. B. Yeats* (New York: Macmillan Co., 1940), p. 185.

2. "Messages from Pinter," *Modern Drama* 10 (May, 1967): 7.

3. "A Critical Analysis of the Stage Plays of Harold Pinter," p. 151.

4. Ibid., p. 139.

5. Martin Esslin, *The Theatre of the Absurd*, p. 208.

6. Introduction to "The Bacchae," in *Euripides V*, The Complete Greek Tragedies, eds. David Grene and Richmond Lattimore (Chicago: University of Chicago Press, 1959), p. 149.

7. Ibid., p. 114.

8. "The Mythos of Autumn: Tragedy," in *Tragedy: Vision and Form*, ed. Robert W. Corrigan, p. 167.

9. Ibid.

10. *Totem and Taboo*, p. 195.

11. *Tragedy, Myth and Mystery*, p. 121.

12. Ibid., p. 128.

13. *The Golden Bough*, p. 668.

14. Wylie Sypher, Introduction to *Comedy*, by George Meredith, p. 230.

15. Ibid.

16. Ibid., p. 228.

17. *Euripides V*, p. 152.

18. Esslin, *Theatre of the Absurd*, p. 207.

19. "The Bacchae," in *Euripides V*, trans. William Arrowsmith, The Complete Greek Tragedies, eds. David Grene and Richmond Lattimore, p. 160.

20. *The Origin of Attic Comedy*, p. 100.

21. P. 317.

22. *Harold Pinter*, p. 31.

23. Curtiss M. Brooks, "The Mythic Pattern in *Waiting for Godot*," *Modern Drama* 9 (December, 1966): 296.

24. John Morrow, lecture given at Ohio State University, 24 May 1967.

25. Brooks, "The Mythic Pattern in *Waiting for Godot*," p. 293.

Chapter 4

1. *The Territorial Imperative: A Personal Inquiry into the Animal Origins of Property and Nations* (New York: Atheneum, 1966), p. 95.

2. "The Examination," in *The Collection" and "The Lover*" (London: Metheun & Co., 1963), p. 89. All subsequent quotations from "The Examination" are from this edition.

3. Quoted by Martin Esslin, *The Theatre of the Absurd*, p. 199.

4. *The Golden Bough*, p. 823.

5. P. 3.

6. Ibid., p. 170.

7. Ronald Hayman is impressed with the similarity between battles for possession of place and woman in Pinter's plays and animal behavior described by Konrad Lorenz in his book, *On Aggression* (Hayman, *Harold Pinter*, p. 78). N. Tinbergen, professor of animal behavior in the department of zoology at the University of Oxford in England, speaks with respect of Lorenz's controversial book in a recent article, "On War and Peace in Animals and Man" (*Science*, 28 June 1968), and considers it a likely hypothesis "that man still carries with him the animal heritage of group territoriality" (p. 1414). He might be writing about Pinter in his article when he suggests that gestures and signals often accomplish more than speech does for communication. He suggests that "many nonscientists, particularly novelists and actors, intuitively understand our sign language much better that we scientists do" (p. 1415).

8. Harold Pinter, "The Dwarfs," in *Three Plays: "A Slight Ache," "The Collection," "The Dwarfs*" (New York: Grove Press, Evergreen Books, 1962), p. 87.

9. Quoted by Henry Hewes in "Probing Pinter's Plays," *Saturday Review*, 8 April 1967, p. 97.

10. *Birth and Rebirth*, p. 130.

11. Daniel Curley, "A Night in the Fun House," *Pinter's Optics*, p. 1.

12. *Anger and After*, p. 288.

13. Harold Pinter, "The Basement," in *"The Lover," "Tea Party," "The Basement*": Two Plays and a Film Script by Harold Pinter (New York: Grove Press, Evergreen Books, 1967), p. 106.

14. Philip Oakes, "Masterly Who's Whose," *Sunday Telegraph*, 17 November 1963.

15. Arnold P. Hinchliffe, *Harold Pinter*, p. 131.

16. " 'The Servant': Notes on the Film," publicity release from Associate British-Pathe in London. Examined at the Library of the British Film Institute.

17. "The Servant," *Sunday Telegraph*, September, 1964.

18. Harold Pinter, "The Black and White," in *"A Night Out," "Night School," "Revue Sketches*": Early Plays by Harold Pinter (New York: Grove Press, Evergreen Books, 1967), pp. 96.

19. "The Last to Go," ibid., pp. 101-2.

20. BBC Third Program portrayal of Pinter sketch, 26 May 1964, recorded by The Sound Institute, Ltd., in London and listened to through the courtesy of the Institute.

21. Ronald Bryden, *Observer*, 2 February 1967.

22. Ibid.

23. Malpas, "A Critical Analysis of the Stage Plays of Harold Pinter," p. 215.

24. Harold Pinter, "The Caretaker," *"The Caretaker" and "The Dumb Waiter"* (New York: Grove Press, Evergreen Books, 1961), p. 12. All subsequent quotations from "The Caretaker" are from this edition.

25. Harold Pinter, "Trouble in the Works," in *"A Night Out," "Night School," "Revue Sketches": Early Plays by Harold Pinter* (New York: Grove Press, Evergreen Books, 1967), p. 92. All subsequent quotations from "Trouble in the Works" are from this edition.

26. *Theatre of the Absurd*, pp. 213-14.

27. *The Territorial Imperative*, p. 170.

28. Malpas, "A Critical Analysis of the Stage Plays of Harold Pinter," p. 207.

29. Richard Schechner, "Puzzling Pinter," *Tulane Drama Review* 11 (Winter, 1966): 181.

30. Arnold P. Hinchliffe, *Harold Pinter*, p. 88.

31. "The Plot-within-the-Plot: Harold Pinter's *The Caretaker*." Paper presented at S.A.A. Convention, 8 December 1967, Los Angeles, California.

32. Ibid., pp. 5-8.

33. *The Theatre of the Absurd*, p. 211.

34. Ibid.

35. "Straightforward Mysticism," *Commonweal*, 27 October 1961, p. 123.

36. Walter Kerr, *Harold Pinter*, p. 26.

37. Interview with Clive Donner, 20 August 1967.

38. Arnold P. Hinchliffe, *Harold Pinter*, p. 100.

39. Interview with Clive Donner, 20 August 1967.

40. Ibid.

41. When I remarked to Mr. Donner in my interview with him that the "van" scene in "The Caretaker" seemed especially brutal, he suggested that the point of comedy is brutality and that Pinter had noted in the course of production on the film, "If it's not funny, its nothing."

42. The ritual action of the film is enhanced by the visual presence of winter in the snow, which helped to underline the play's identification of Davies with age and winter.

43. Quoted by Arnold P. Hinchliffe, *Harold Pinter*, p. 99.

Chapter 5

1. *Three Tragedies*, The Complete Greek Tragedies, eds. David Grene and Richmond Lattimore (Chicago: The University of Chicago Press, 1960), p. 152.

2. Interview with Martin Esslin, 24 August 1967.

3. Quoted by Henry Hewes, "Probing Pinter's Play," *Saturday Review*, 8 April 1967, p. 56.

4. As in Ernest Jones's study *Hamlet and Oedipus* (New York: W. W. Norten, 1949).

5. *Totem and Taboo*, p. 202.

6. Ibid., pp. 196-97.

7. Ibid., p. 197.

8. Gilbert Murray, "Hamlet and Orestes," in *The Critical Performance: An Anthology of American and British Literary Criticism of Our Century*, ed. Stanley Edgar Hyman (New York: Vintage Books, 1956), p. 36.

9. Ibid.

10. Ibid., p. 37.

11. Ibid., p. 39.

12. Ibid., pp. 39-40.

13. *Totem and Taboo*, p. 97.

14. Ibid., pp. 96-97.

15. Harold Pinter, "A Night Out," in *"A Night Out," "Night School," "Revue Sketches": Early Plays by Harold Pinter* (New York: Grove Press, Evergreen Books, 1967), p. 6. All subsequent quotations from "A Night Out" are from this edition.

16. Roger Manvell, "A Decade of Harold Pinter," *Humanist* 132 (April, 1967): 115.

17. *The Golden Bough*, p. 823.

18. Quoted by Arnold Hinchliffe, *Harold Pinter*, p. 138.

19. Harold Pinter, "Tea Party," in *"The Lover," "Tea Party," "The Basement": Two Plays and a Film Script by Harold Pinter* (New York:

Grove Press, Evergreen Books, 1967), p. 44. All subsequent quotations from "Tea Party" are from this adition.

20. *Harold Pinter*, p. 60.

21. Ibid.

22. *Harold Pinter*, p. 138.

23. Walter Kerr, *Harold Pinter*, p. 29.

24. Ibid., p. 35.

25. Ibid., p. 36.

26. Interview with Martin Esslin, 24 August 1967.

27. Harold Clurman, *The Naked Image*, pp. 109-10.

28. Harold Pinter, "The Lover," in *"The Lover," "Tea Party," "The Basement"*: *Two Plays and a Film Script by Harold Pinter* (New York: Grove Press, Evergreen Books, 1967), p. 5. All subsequent quotations from "The Lover" are from this edition.

29. Interview with Roger Manvell, 17 August 1967.

30. "Putting up with Love," *Sunday Telegraph*, 19 July 1964.

31. Alexander Walker, "Magnificent, Yes—and Now I Know Why . . . ," *Evening Standard*, 16 July 1964.

32. Harold Pinter, *The Homecoming* (New York: Grove Press, Evergreen Books, 1966), p. 42. All subsequent quotations from *The Homecoming* are from this edition.

33. Personal communication.

34. Quoted by Henry Hewes, "Probing Pinter's Plays," *Saturday Review*, 8 April 1967, p. 56.

35. *Myth and Reality*, p. 30.

36. "Puzzling Pinter," p. 183.

37. Quoted by Henry Hewes, "Probing Pinter's Plays," p. 56.

Chapter 6

1. Harold Pinter, "Writing for Myself," *Twentieth Century* 169 (February, 1969): 174.

2. Interview with Lawrence Pressman, 21 August 1967. All subsequent references to Pressman refer to this interview.

3. An interview with Pinter by Kenneth Tynan on the B.B.C., 28 October 1960. Heard on a recording at the British Institute of Recorded Sound.

4. Interview with Joan Kemp-Welch, 19 August 1967. All subsequent references to Miss Kemp-Welch refer to this interview.

5. Interview with Martin Esslin, 24 August 1967. All subsequent references to Mr. Esslin refer to this interview.

6. Quoted by Joan Barthel, "If You Didn't Know It Was by Pinter," *New York Times*, 10 October 1967.

7. Interview with Clive Donner, 21 August 1967.

8. Quoted by Malpas, "A Critical Analysis of the Stage Plays of Harold Pinter," p. 36.

9. Quoted in *Saturday Review*, 8 April 1967.

10. "Saturn Eats His Children," *New Republic*, 28 January 1967, p. 36.

11. *Christian Century*, 8 September 1965.

12. "The Theatre," *Nation*, 23 January 1967, p. 123.

13. Ibid.

14. An undated review of *The Birthday Party* in Joan Kemp-Welch's personal scrapbook.

15. Giles Jacob, "Joseph Losey or the Camera Calls," *Sight and Sound* 34 (Spring, 1966): 65.

16. Tom Milne, "Two Films I: *Accident*," *Sight and Sound* 35 (Spring, 1967): 59.

17. *Times* (London), 28 July 1967.

18. *Daily Telegraph*, 28 July 1967.

19. *Times* (London), 30 July 1967.

20. *New York Times*, 27 August 1967.

21. Ibid.

22. Ibid.

23. Conversation with Pinter at a preview of *Macbeth* in Stratford, England, 1967.

Chapter 7

1. Quoted by Ann Saddlemyer in "The Heroic Discipline of the Looking Glass: W. B. Yeats's Search for Dramatic Design," in *The World of William Butler Yeats*, eds. Robin Skelton and Ann Saddlemyer, rev. ed. (Seattle: University of Washington Press, 1967), p. 72.

2. Interviewed in *Isis*, 1 February 1964, p. 19.

3. Ibid.

4. Interviewed on the BBC by Owen Webster, 2 June 1960. Heard on a recording through the courtesy of Mr. Martin Esslin at the BBC.

5. Ibid.

6. Interviewed by Lawrence M. Bensky in *The Playwrights Speak*, p. 184.

7. *Themis*, ed. Jane Ellen Harrison, p. xix.

8. Interviewed on the BBC by Kenneth Tynan, 28 October 1960. Heard on a recording through the courtesy of Mr. Martin Esslin at the BBC.

9. *Harold Pinter*, p. 5.

10. "Comedy," in *Comedy: Meaning and Form*, ed. Robert W. Corrigan, p. 16.

Chapter 8

1. Pinter as quoted on the paper cover of *"Landscape" and "Silence"* (London: Methuen & Co., Ltd., 1969).

2. Ibid.

BIBLIOGRAPHY

Works by Pinter

"*Birthday Party, The*" and "*The Room*": *Two Plays by Harold Pinter.* New York: Grove Press, Evergreen Books, 1961.
"*Caretaker, The*" and "*The Dumb Waiter*": *Two Plays by Harold Pinter.* New York: Grove Press, Evergreen Books, 1961.
"*Collection, The*" and "*The Lover.*" London: Methuen & Co., Ltd., 1963. (This includes the short story, "The Examination.")
Homecoming, The. New York: Grove Press, Evergreen Books, 1966.
"*Landscape*" and *Silence.*" London: Methuen & Co., Ltd., 1969. (This includes the dramatic sketch "Night.")
"*Lover, The,*" "*Tea Party,*" "*The Basement*": *Two Plays and a Film Script by Harold Pinter.* New York: Grove Press, Evergreen Books, 1967.
"*Night Out, A,*" "*Night School,*" "*Revue Sketches*": *Early Plays by Harold Pinter.* New York: Grove Press, Evergreen Books, 1967.
"*Quiller Memorandum, The.*" Film Script. London: Rank Productions, 1966. (I was able to examine the unpublished film script through the courtesy of the Society of Film and Television Arts, London.)
"*Slight Ache, A*" and *Other Plays.* London: Methuen & Co., Ltd., 1969. (This includes A *Slight Ache*, A *Night Out, The Dwarfs*, and the following revue sketches: "Trouble in the Works," "The Black and White," "Request Stop," "Last to Go," and "Applicant.")
"*Tea Party*" and *Other Plays.* London: Methuen & Co., 1967. (This includes *Tea Party, The Basement*, and *Night School.*)
Three Plays by Harold Pinter. New York: Grove Press, Evergreen Books, 1962. (This includes A *Slight Ache, The Collection*, and *The Dwarfs.*)
"*Writing for Myself.*" *Twentieth Century* 169 (February, 1969): 172-75.

Other Works Cited

Bensky, Lawrence. "Interview with Harold Pinter." In *Modern British Dramatists: A Collection of Critical Essays*, edited by John Russell Brown. Twentieth Century Views. New Jersey: Prentice-Hall, 1968.
Bensky, Lawrence. "Interview with Harold Pinter." In *The Playwrights*

166

Speak, edited by Walter Wagner. New York: Dell Publishing Co., A Delta Book, 1967.

Bidney, David. "Myth, Symbolism, and Truth." In *Myth and Literature: Contemporary Theory and Practice*, edited by John B. Vickery. Lincoln: University of Nebraska Press, 1966.

Brooks, Curtiss M. "The Mythic Pattern in Waiting for Godot." *Modern Drama* 9 (December, 1966): 292-99.

Brown, John Russell. Introduction to *Modern British Dramatists: A Collection of Critical Essays*, edited by John Russell Brown. Twentieth Century Views. New Jersey: Prentice-Hall, 1968.

Brustein, Robert. "A Naturalism of the Grotesque." In *Seasons of Discontent: Dramatic Opinions, 1959-65*. New York: Simon & Schuster, 1965.

————. "Saturn Eats His Children." *New Republic*, 28 January 1967, pp. 34-36.

Campbell, Joseph. "Bias and Mythos: Prolegomena to a Science of Mythology." In *Myth and Literature: Contemporary Theory and Practice*, edited by John B. Vickery. Lincoln: University of Nebraska Press, 1966.

Clurman, Harold. *The Naked Image: Observations on the Modern Theatre*. New York: The Macmillan Co., 1966.

————. "The Theatre." *The Nation*, 23 January 1967, pp. 122-23.

Cornford, Francis. *The Origin of Attic Comedy*. London: Edward Arnold, 1914.

Curley, Daniel. "A Night in the Fun House." *Pinter's Optics*, Midwest Monographs, Series 1, No. 1. Urbana, Illinois: Depot Press, 1967. Pp. 1-2.

Eliade, Mircea. *Birth and Rebirth: The Religious Meaning of Initiation in Human Culture*. Translated by Willard R. Trask. New York: Harper & Brothers, 1958.

————. *Myth and Reality*. Translated by Willard R. Trask. New York: Harper & Row, 1963.

Esslin, Martin. "Godot and His Children: The Theatre of Samuel Beckett and Harold Pinter." In *Modern British Dramatists: A Collection of Critical Essays*, edited by John Russell Brown. Twentieth Century Views. New Jersey: Prentice-Hall, 1968.

————. *The Theatre of the Absurd*. New York: Doubleday & Co., Anchor Books, 1961.

Frazer, Sir James George. *The Golden Bough*. Abr. ed. in 1 vol. New York: The Macmillan Co., 1951.

Freud, Sigmund. *Totem and Taboo: Resemblances Between the Psychic Lives of Savages and Neurotics*. Translated by A. A. Brill. New York: Random House, Vintage Books, 1946.

Fry, Christopher. "Comedy." In *Comedy: Meaning and Form*, edited by Robert W. Corrigan. California: Chandler Publishing Co., 1965.

Frye, Northrop. *Anatomy of Criticism: Four Essays*. 1957. Reprint ed. New York: Atheneum, 1966.

——. "The Archetypes of Literature." In *Myth and Literature: Contemporary Theory and Practice*, edited by John B. Vickery. Lincoln: University of Nebraska Press, 1966.

——. "The Mythos of Autumn: Tragedy." In *Tragedy: Vision and Form*, edited by Robert W. Corrigan. California: Chandler Publishing Co., 1965.

Gilman, Richard. "Straightforward Mysticism." *Commonweal*, 27 October 1961, pp. 122-23.

Halton, Kathleen. "Pinter." *Vogue*, 1 October 1967, p. 194.

Harrison, Jane Ellen. *Themis: A Study of the Social Origins of Greek Religion*. Cambridge: At the University Press, 1912.

Hathorn, Richard Y. *Tragedy, Myth and Mystery*. Indiana: University of Indiana Press, 1963.

Hayman, Ronald. *Harold Pinter*. Contemporary Playwrights. London: Heinemann, Heinemann Educational Books, 1968.

Hewes, Henry. "Disobedience, Civil and Uncivil." *Saturday Review*, 28 October 1967, pp. 46-47. Copyright 1967 Saturday Review, Inc.

——. "Probing Pinter's Plays." *Saturday Review*, 8 April 1967, p. 56.

Hinchliffe, Arnold P. *Harold Pinter*. Twayne's English Authors Series. New York: Twayne Publishers, 1967.

Hyman, Stanley Edgar. "The Ritual View of Myth and Mythic." In *Myth and Literature: Contemporary Theory and Practice*, edited by John B. Vickery. Lincoln: University of Nebraska Press, 1966.

Isis, 1 February 1964, entire issue on Joseph Losey.

Jacob, Giles. "Joseph Losey or the Camera Calls." *Sight and Sound* 34 (Spring, 1966): 62-67.

James, E. O. *Seasonal Feasts and Festivals*. New York: Barnes & Noble, 1961.

Kerr, Walter. *Harold Pinter*. Columbia Essays on Modern Writers. New York: Columbia University Press, 1967.

Kluckhohn, Clyde. "Myth and Ritual: A General Theory." In *Myth and Literature: Contemporary Theory and Practice*, edited by John B. Vickery. Lincoln: University of Nebraska Press, 1966.

"Land of No Holds Barred," *Time*, 13 January 1967, p. 43.

Manvell, Roger. "The Decade of Harold Pinter," *Humanist* 132 (April, 1967): 112-15.

Milne, Tom. "Two Films I: *Accident.*" *Sight and Sound* 35 (Spring, 1967): 57-59.

Murray, Gilbert. "Excursus on the Ritual Forms Preserved in Greek Tragedy." In *Themis: A Study of the Social Origins of Greek Religion,* edited by Jane Ellen Harrison. Cambridge: At the University Press, 1912.

Nelson, Hugh. "The Homecoming: Kith and Kin." In *Modern British Dramatists: A Collection of Critical Essays,* edited by John Russell Brown. Twentieth Century Views. New Jersey: Prentice-Hall, 1968.

Schechner, Richard. "Puzzling Pinter." *Tulane Drama Review* 11 (Winter, 1966): 176-84.

Smith, Warren Sylvester. *Christian Century,* 8 September 1965, pp. 1096-97.

Sypher, Wylie. Introduction to *Comedy,* by George Meredith. New York: Doubleday & Co., 1956.

Taylor, John Russell. *Anger and After: A Guide to the New English Drama.* Maryland: Penguin Books, A Pelican Book, 1963.

Vickery, John B. Introduction to *Myth and Literature: Contemporary Theory and Practice,* edited by John B. Vickery. Lincoln: University of Nebraska Press, 1966.

———. *"The Golden Bough:* Impact and Archetype." In *Myth and Symbol: Critical Approaches and Applications,* edited by Bernice Slote. Lincoln: University of Nebraska Press, 1963.

Vos, Nelvin. *The Drama of Comedy: Victim and Victor.* Virginia: John Knox Press, 1966.

Walker, Augusta. "Messages from Pinter." *Modern Drama* 10 (May, 1967): 1-10.

Wimsatt, William R., Jr., and Brooks, Cleanth. *Literary Criticism: A Short History.* New York: Alfred A. Knopf, 1946.

Manuscript Sources

Busch, Lloyd. "The Plot-within-the-Plot: Harold Pinter's *The Caretaker.*" Paper given at an S.A.A. Convention, 8 December 1967, Los Angeles, California.

Frisch, J. E. "Ironic Theatre: Techniques of Irony in the Plays of Samuel Beckett, Eugene Ionesco, Harold Pinter and Jean Genet." Ph.D. dissertation, University of Wisconsin, 1965.

Malpas, Edward Reginald Howard. "A Critical Analysis of the Stage Plays of Harold Pinter." Ph.D. dissertation, University of Wisconsin, 1965.

Pierce, Roger. "Three Play Analyses." Ph.D. dissertation, University of Iowa, 1969.

INDEX

Absurdist drama, 6, 7, 8, 38–39

Accident, The (film), 116–18, 126, 138

Alazon, 51, 52, 55–58, 84. See also Eiron; Ritual; Scapegoat

Ardrey, Robert, 67, 81. See also Territorial Imperative, The

Aristotle, 8, 19, 133

Bacchae, The (Euripides): analysis of, 49–52; clue to celebration in Pinter's plays of, 138–39; compared to A Slight Ache, 49–52, 54, 57, 62, 63; Dionysus in, 49, 52, 54–57, 63, 139

Basement, The, 68, 73, 98

Beckett, Samuel, 7, 12, 20, 139; Waiting for Godot, 12, 19, 20, 24, 27, 33, 63, 139

Birthday Party, The, 4, 5, 20, 21, 94, 137–38; analysis of, 23–39; blindness in, 139; compared with (A Slight Ache, 47, 49, 62, 64; A Night Out, 97; Tea Party, 100, 102; The Bacchae, 52; The Caretaker, 77; The Golden Bough, 67; The Room, 72); oedipal tension in, 92

Cambridge school of anthropologists, 13, 134. See also Frazer, Sir James; Golden Bough, The; Harrison, Jane Ellen; Murray, Gilbert

Caretaker, The, 20, 68, 122, 137; analysis of, 76–87; compared with The Birthday Party, 44;

compared with The Homecoming, 114; film of, 87–89; women in, 91, 92, 95

Collection, The, 92, 95, 136; analysis of, 102–4

Dionysus. See Bacchae, The

Donner, Clive, 87–89, 121–24

Dumb Waiter, The, 5, 20, 21, 23; analysis of, 39–44; compared with (A Slight Ache, 47, 64; The Birthday Party, 86; The Room, 72)

Dwarfs, The: analysis of, 68–70; compared with A Slight Ache, 68–70; compared with The Caretaker, 86, 87, 95

Eiron, 51, 52, 55, 56, 58, 63. See also Alazon; Ritual; Scapegoat

Eliade, Mircea, 38, 115

Eliot, T. S., 16, 33, 69, 70, 147

Esslin Martin, 79, 85, 86, 92, 121, 123, 124; on absurdists, 6, 7; on A Slight Ache, 49

Euripides. See Bacchae, The

"Examination, The" (short story), 65, 66, 73

Fertility goddess, role of: in A Slight Ache, 53, 54, 58, 62, 104, 134; in Landscape, 143; in The Accident, 116–17; in The Bacchae, 51, 62; in The Basement, 98; in The Birthday Party, 2, 5, 33, 97; in The Collection, 103–4;